MIND FIELDS

MIND FIELDS

Reflections on the Science of Mind and Brain

Malcolm Jeeves

Baker Books

A Division of Baker Book House Co.
Grand Rapids, Michigan 49516

© New College University of NSW, 1993

Published 1994 by Baker Books
a division of Baker Book House Company
P.O. Box 6287, Grand Rapids, MI 49516-6287
with permission of Anzea Publishers.

British Library Cataloguing in Publication Data
A catalogue record for this book is available from the British Library.

Australian ISBN 0 85892 525 7
UK ISBN 0 85111 434 2
US ISBN 0-8010-5227-0

Foreword

An address by Professor L M Birt

Sir Lawrence and Lady Street, Your Grace and Mrs Robinson, Professor and Mrs Jeeves, distinguished guests, ladies and gentlemen.

Sir Lawrence remarked a moment ago that tonight might recall the long and fruitful association between the Christian religion and university education. That reminded me that the Master and I have shared over the time that he has been in the University of New South Wales an enthusiasm for the educational writings of John Henry Newman; and that then suggested to me that there was a somewhat ironic aspect to this evening's activity. Two of Newman's most significant beliefs, I think, about university education were firstly, that it must emphasise what he called the 'circle of knowledge', the fact that all human knowledge must eventually be interconnected and the balance struck between the various bodies of knowledge which make up the different disciplines. The second element that I recall is that theology is one of the subjects which any university worthy of the name should include in its curriculum, because theology is the 'queen of the sciences', concerned with human values and human values in relation to divine purpose and divine understanding. I say that this is an ironic recollection because these two aspects of uni-

versity education on which he laid such stress have almost
disappeared from a large, modern university such as this one.
The size and, I think, the specialisation of knowledge in our
academic disciplines means that the 'circle of knowledge' notion
has almost become a romantic fiction. Each discipline beavers
away in its own narrow field, and only very occasionally looks
across the boundaries to wonder what is going on in another
part of the academic endeavour. Newman would, I think, be
horrified and astonished and feel impoverished in our environment; we don't teach theology—very few Australian universities
do. In other words, we ignore in our formal activities, to a very
large extent, the considerations which give value, purpose, direction and finally personal and institutional meaning to human
lives and human activities. I was, therefore, delighted when
Bruce Kaye told me that New College was going to do something to remedy this deficiency in the University of New South
Wales because this series of lectures, as I understand it, will
over the years explore the interaction between different disciplines, will look out across discipline boundaries and will
recall the fact that finally all education must have a bearing on
human values and the relationship between the human and the
divine. So it is a very important occasion, not only because this
is the inaugural lecture in a very important series, but because
the direction which it proposes to take is a very important one
indeed for any university and perhaps especially for a modern
Australian university.

I would like to congratulate Dr Kaye and his colleagues in
having the courage and the wisdom to establish these lectures.
I am also delighted that the first lecture in this series should be
given by someone with a long and distinguished career in
neuropsychology. Professor Jeeves is Professor of Psychology
in the University of St Andrews, was Professor of Psychology
in the University of Adelaide, and is a very distinguished scholar.
Let me mention the last two of his publications as an indication
of the kind of work that he is doing; namely *Free To Be
Different*, in 1984, and then, very significantly, *Behavioural
Sciences—A Christian Perspective*, also in 1984. He is going to
consider, in this inaugural series, the theme *Man Under His Own
Microscope*, looking at how the scientific study of man has

affected our knowledge of ourselves as human beings, and the implications of that study for human society and for religious and other human values. In his first lecture, Professor Jeeves will 'map out the territory'; and he will go on then to an exploration of that map in the succeeding four lectures. I have very much pleasure indeed in inviting Professor Malcolm Jeeves to deliver this first lecture in the series, *Man Under His Own Microscope.*

Professor L M Birt
Vice Chancellor and Principal
University of New South Wales

Contents

Preface

In his letter inviting me to give the inaugural series of *New College Lectures*, Dr Bruce Kaye, Master of New College, University of New South Wales, asked if I would 'take up some aspect of contemporary society and to reflect upon it'. At a time of intense research activity and exciting advances in the neurosciences in general, and in neuropsychology in particular, I focused my lectures on selected aspects of what is happening in these areas and with which, through my own research, I am familiar. That led me to talk about diverse lines of evidence which have been widely interpreted as indicating a steadily tightening link between mind and brain. This is an issue which some see as having wider implications. For example, what does it say about our deeply held belief in human freedom of choice and action and about our traditional views of human nature?

Aware of the range of interpretations already given to the results of some of the research findings, it also provided an opportunity to raise and comment on wider issues. For example, of how a scientist's presuppositions—sometimes called his 'world view'—may influence his construction and interpretation of the scientific model he favours—sometimes called a 'word picture'. Thus whilst discussing the science of the mind/brain link I illustrated how differing interpretations of the same data were offered and could validly be held by equally well-informed and competent neuroscientists. I asked, for example, how they reconciled their personal convictions that they were indeed free to choose what to study, how to study it and what to make of their data, with their assumptions that mental events, including their own, were embedded in the workings of a physical system, the brain, the components of which operated according to the laws of physics and chemistry. In addition, since New College is a Christian foundation, it seemed appropriate to ask how the picture of human nature emerging from psychology and neuroscience relates to traditional Christian views on the same topic.

This book is an expanded version of some of the material covered in my lectures. The first four chapters provide a brief historical background to the mind/brain linkage and trace out the story of the tightening of the mind/brain link and how ideas about localisation of function in the brain have changed and developed over the centuries. Whilst the close correlation of mental processes and brain processes is beyond dispute, the best way to think about, model and understand that correlation is still very much an open question under lively debate. Later chapters remind us that no man is an island and that the environments, physical and social, affect the development and working of the brain.

The final three chapters deal with wider non-scientific issues. Chapter six notes that there are special problems when people study people, as distinct from people studying inanimate objects. Chapter seven looks in more general terms at how our personal 'world views' relate to the 'word pictures' of our science. In the final chapter we ask, 'What then is man?' (and by the way, the word *man* is used throughout in its generic sense to denote man and woman). In so doing we touch upon some of the issues which seem naturally to arise in the minds of Christians when they begin to appreciate the tightness of the mind/brain link and speculate about what it might imply for some long held beliefs such as life after physical death.

The mind/brain link

An enduring puzzle

A current widespread concern

It is likely that every reader of this book can think of a relative or friend who suffers from an illness in which their mind is affected. In many of the instances that come to mind it seems that the mental problems are linked to changes in the structure of the brain. Whether we think of the results of a stroke, of Parkinson's disease, Alzheimer's disease, some forms of schizophrenia, some forms of depression or possibly some neurotic illnesses, the evidence points more and more to the pressing need to understand the biological basis of our mental life.

These are exciting times. Whilst we must be careful not to raise false hopes by implying that a new dawn is around the corner, nevertheless so much research is going on at the moment into the mind/brain link that a cautious optimism is justified. There is hope that some of the most distressing and intractable illnesses, such as schizophrenia, will yield to the onslaught of sustained scientific research within a decade or two. The financial support given to such work increases all the time. For example, in the UK only recently the Medical Research Council funded an initiative in the field of brain and behaviour. In the

USA a Senate Committee labelled the 1990s *The Decade of the Brain*. Their report declared . . .

> it is estimated that fifty million Americans are affected each year by disorders and disabilities that involve the brain, including the major mental illnesses; inherited and degenerative diseases; stroke; epilepsy; addictive disorders; injury resulting from prenatal events, environmental neurotoxins and trauma; and speech, language, hearing and other cognitive disorders;
>
> the people of the Nation should be aware of the exciting research advances on the brain and of the availability of effective treatment of disorders and disabilities that affect the brain;
>
> scientific information on the brain is amassing at an enormous rate, and the field of computer and information sciences has reached a level of sophistication sufficient to handle neuroscience data in a manner that would be maximally useful to both researchers and clinicians dealing with brain function and dysfunction;
>
> fundamental discoveries at the molecular and cellular levels of the organization of the brain are clarifying the role of the brain in translating neurophysiologic events into behavior, thought, and emotion;
>
> the study of the brain involves the multidisciplinary efforts of scientists from such diverse areas as physiology, biochemistry, psychology, psychiatry, molecular biology, anatomy, medicine, genetics, and many others working together toward the common goals of better understanding the structure of the brain and how it affects our development, health and behavior . . .[1]

Whilst research in the area of mind/brain relations has a long and patchy history, today, in the second half of the 20th century, the pace is rapidly accelerating.

The need for a balanced view
The mind/brain unity does not function in a vacuum. The physical and social environments in which we live affect the mind/brain unity that we are. So, whilst the major concern of this book is to give the flavour of what current research is revealing about the complexities of the mind/brain link, it must all be set in the context of the clear recognition of the importance of environment. As Lipowski pointed out in his First Distinguished Member Lecture of the Canadian Psychiatric Associa-

tion, the temptation always is to veer to one extreme or the other in discussing the mind/brain link. As a psychiatrist, he argued that neither brainless nor mindless psychiatry could do justice to mental illness and to the treatment of patients. He emphasised that '. . . a person, viewed as a mind/body complex, is in constant interaction with the environment. It follows that both study of mental illness and clinical practice need to take into account the psychological, the biological, and the social aspects. These three aspects are not mutually reducible and are indispensable for the understanding and treatment of the individual patient.'[2] We shall return to this issue from time to time, but for now I wish to make it clear that all that is written about the mind/brain link is in the full recognition of the importance of the environment.

The need for a circumscribed objective

In this book I sketch out with examples something of what is happening in mind/brain research so as to convey the flavour of the field. I also explore some of the implications that this may have for some of our traditional non-scientific views of ourselves and by implication of other people. If, for example, my mental activity depends so intimately on the physical state of my brain, and if my brain is a physically determinate system, then what am I to make of some of my most cherished convictions about my personal freedom and responsibility?

This is not a philosophical book. I am not a philosopher. I am a working scientist but inevitably the implications of what I do raise wider issues. Even so, I believe we can enthusiastically welcome and applaud the way in which research on mind and brain is progressing at the present time.

Any interpretation of what is happening does not occur in a vacuum. It is inextricably bound up with what has been called one's 'world view'. For me it is a Christian one. This being so, in the final chapter I shall explore the implications of some of the models emerging from neuroscience for some of the traditional Christian views of man. I shall argue that many of the underlying presuppositions which guide research into the mind/brain link and which inform its interpretations are shared by Christians, humanists and those in other religious traditions.

Three incidents to set the scene

1783

By the year 1783, the famous English author, Dr Samuel Johnson, was already markedly overweight. In his diary he records how he spent the afternoon of June 16th sitting for his portrait. The artist was the somewhat untalented sister of Sir Joshua Reynolds. (It was said that her paintings made most people laugh and her brother cry.) At the end of the afternoon sitting, Dr Johnson walked a considerable distance from Miss Frances Reynolds' studio to his home. According to his own account of what then happened, he went to sleep at his usual hour but awoke around three o'clock the following morning and discovered to his horror and surprise that he could no longer speak. He records how he immediately tested his mental faculties by trying to compose a prayer in Latin verse. Having succeeded in doing this he then tried to loosen his powers of speech by drinking a little wine, thereby violating his recently acquired habits of temperance. The wine had an effect, but rather than releasing his speech it put him back to sleep.

When he reawoke after sunrise he still couldn't speak. He found, however, that he could understand what others said to him and he could still write, although his penmanship and composition were somewhat defective. He summoned his physicians who, having examined him, prescribed the accepted treatment of that time. It was to inflict blisters on each side of his throat up to the ear, one on the head, and one on the back, together with regular does of salts of hartshorn (today we would call this ammonium carbonate).

He was fortunate to be in the hands of one of London's leading physicians, a Dr Heberden, who predicted a speedy recovery. His confidence was justified. Indeed, the therapeutic procedure was so successful that Dr Johnson's speech began to return within a day or two, proceeded smoothly over the next month, and even the mild disorders in writing became less. Whilst he was left with a slight difficulty in speaking, it was to other causes that he finally succumbed later the next year. The point of relating this incident is to note that in the 18th century the leading physicians seemingly saw no link between something wrong with the ability to speak and what was going on in the brain. Instead, they 'treated' peripheral structures located in the neck and throat believing that here was the physical substrate of speech. Brain events and mind events were not linked.

1975

The second incident occurs nearly two centuries later and is recorded in Dr Oliver Sacks' book, *The Man who Mistook his Wife for a Hat*.[3] Jimmie is admitted to a home for the aged near New York City and brings with him a note which says that he is 'helpless, demented, confused and disoriented'. Dr Sacks describes Jimmie as fine-looking with a curly bush of grey hair; a healthy and handsome man of 49 years. He is friendly, cheerful and warm. The conversation runs like this:

'Hiya Doc. Nice morning. Do I take this chair here?'

'What year is this, Mr G?' asks the neurologist.

''45 man, what do you mean? We've won the war, FDR is dead, Trueman's at the helm, there are great times ahead.'

'And you, Jimmie, how old would you be?'

'Why, I guess I'm 19, Doc. I'll be 20 next birthday.'

Dr Sacks further describes how on an impulse for which he has never forgiven himself, he thrust a mirror towards Jimmie and said, 'Here, look in the mirror and tell me what you see. Is that a 19 year old looking out from the mirror? At this Jimmie turned ashen and gripped the sides of his chair. 'Jesus Christ,' he whispered, 'Christ, what's going on? What's happened to me? Is this a nightmare? Am I crazy? Is this a joke?' and he became frantic, panicked.

'It's okay, Jimmie,' the neurologist said soothingly, 'it's just a mistake, nothing to worry about. Hey,' and he took him to the window, 'isn't this a lovely spring day. See the kids there playing basketball.' Jimmie regained his colour and began to smile, and the neurologist left, taking the mirror with him.

Two minutes later he re-entered the room. Jimmie was still by the window, gazing with pleasure at the kids playing baseball. He wheeled round, his face assumed a cheery expression.

'Hiya, Doc,' he said, 'nice morning. You want me to talk? Do I take this chair here?' There was no sign of recognition that he had ever seen the neurologist before.

'Haven't we met before Mr G?' the neurologist asked.

'No, I can't say we have. Quite a beard you've got there. I wouldn't forget you, doctor.'

'Why do you call me "Doc"?'

'Well, you are a doc, ain't you?'

'Yes, but if you haven't met me, how do you know what I am?'

'You talk like a doc. I can see you are a doc.'

'Well, you're right, I am. I am a neurologist here.'

'Neurologist. Hey, there's something wrong with my nerves and here, where's here, what is this place anyhow.'

When tested on standard intelligence tests, Jimmie showed excellent ability. He was quick-witted, observant, logical, could solve complex problems and puzzles without any difficulty, provided they could be done quickly. If time was required, however, he forgot what he was doing. As the neurologist describes it, 'he found in this man an extreme and extraordinary loss of recent memory, so that whatever was said or shown, or done to him, would be forgotten in a few seconds' time.' It wasn't apparently that he failed to register things in memory, but that the memory traces were fugitive in the extreme, and would be erased within a minute and often less. At the end of a gruelling examination, the neurologist described himself as wrung with emotion. 'It was,' he wrote, 'heartbreaking. It was absurd. It was deeply perplexing to think of this man's life lost in limbo, dissolving.' He wrote in his notes, 'He is, as it were, isolated in a single moment of being, with a mote or lacuna of forgetting all round him. He is a man without a past or future, stuck in a constantly changing, meaningless moment.' A subsequent examination by a psychiatrist reported that this patient showed no evidence whatsoever of any hysterical or put-on deficit. His memory deficits he said were organic and permanent and incorrigible.

Oliver Sacks narrates how he wrote to the Russian neuropsychologist, Luria, one of this century's most outstanding neuropsychologists, who had seen similar cases. Luria wrote back,

There are no prescriptions in a case like this. Do whatever your ingenuity and your heart suggests. There is little or no hope of recovery in his memory. A man does not consist of memory alone. He has feeling, will, sensibilities, moral being, matters of which neuropsychology cannot speak, and it is here beyond the realm of an impersonal psychology that you may find ways to touch him and change him . . . Neuropsychologically, there is little or nothing you can do; but in the realm of the individual, there may be much you can do.

Totally baffled by this patient, Oliver Sacks describes how he tended to speak of him instinctively as a spiritual casualty, a lost soul. He wondered if it was possible that Jimmie had really been desouled by a disease. Indeed, he put the question to the sisters in the home where he was staying, 'Do you think he has a soul?' He reports that they were outraged by his question, but could see why he had asked it. Their reply was, 'Watch Jimmie in chapel, and judge for yourself.' He goes on to report how, as he watched him in chapel, he was profoundly moved and impressed because he saw an intensity and steadiness of attention and concentration he had never seen before in him, or thought possible. He watched him kneel and take the sacrament on his tongue, and could not doubt the fullness and totality of communion, the perfect alignment of his spirit with the spirit of the mass. Fully, intensely, he reports, quietly in the quietude of absolute concentration and attention, he entered and partook of the Holy Communion. He was wholly held, absorbed by a feeling. The neurologist in his account goes on, 'Clearly Jimmie found himself, found continuity and reality in the absoluteness of spiritual attention and act. The sisters were right, he did find his soul here,' he goes on, 'so was Luria right, whose words now came back to me, the man does not consist of memory alone. He has feeling, will, sensibility, moral being, it is here, you may touch him and see a profound change. Memory, mental activity, mind alone could not hold him; but moral attention and action could hold him completely.

1986

The third incident is a newspaper report which appeared in August 1986 that Muhammed Ali has been exploring the possibility of what the press calls a brain transplant in order to alleviate his progressive disabilities due to brain damage of a

Parkinsonian kind. Is there such a thing as 'brain transplant'? That surely is science fiction of the worst kind, or is it? We shall return to this in Chapter 3.

Tracing out the story

If you pause and reflect for a moment, the 'obvious' place to localise the mind, if it is to be localised at all, is in the heart. When you think exciting thoughts there is a thumping in the chest. When you think peaceful thoughts your heart is quiet. From what is called a phenomenological point of view then, it seems 'obvious' that the mind resides in the heart. Indeed, it seems as obvious that the mind resides in the heart as it seems that the earth is flat. After all, you can look and look but you do not see the round earth. If you depend just on your experience you must have a good deal of sympathy with the obstinacy of the flat-earthers especially when they were first asked to believe that the earth was round.

True, empirical observations in isolation can lead to several differing conclusions, including the refutation or calling into question of current beliefs. Perhaps the best example of this was when the Dutch sailors sailed off into the sunset and finally returned, not having fallen off the edge of the flat earth, but having circumnavigated the globe. Their experience of the way the earth really is pretty conclusively laid the flat earth theory to rest for most people! Have there, we may ask, been similar empirical observations of the mind/body link which have prompted radical rethinkings of the nature of man?

Down the centuries limited observations seemed to support different theories of the mind/body relationship. In the 5th century BC, Empedocles reasserted the notion that the soul (their word for the mind) dwelt in the heart and in the blood, a theory which was labelled *the cardiovascular theory*. His views, however, did not go unchallenged. At the same time, Alcmaeon of Croton asserted that mental functions are to be located in the brain. His view was labelled *the encephalic view*. These two theories were destined to compete with each other for another 2,000 years.

The great physician, Hippocrates, who lived some time between 460 and 360 BC, adopted the brain or encephalic theory of mind. One of his texts deals extensively with epilepsy and, as is well known, bears the famous title *On the sacred disease*. It makes the brain the interpreter of consciousness as well as the mediator of feelings. It argues that epilepsy is not really a sacred disease but a perfectly natural and understandable disease with natural causes.

Plato and Aristotle in the 4th century BC continued the conflict between the encephalic and cardiovascular theories. Plato seems to have wanted it both ways, locating the immortal soul in the 'marrow' of the head, which presumably is the brain, but locating the passions between the neck and the midriff. He also puts the appetites between the midriff and the navel. Aristotle, for his part, quite unambiguously localised the soul in the heart. He had reasons for his views and he still had a role for the brain. Being a good biologist he decided it must serve some function. Noticing that it was moist and cool to the touch he concluded that it refrigerated the blood. Aristotle's views were passed on through the Stoic philosophers to one of the early Church fathers, Tertullian, whilst the encephalic theory continued to survive through one of Rome's outstanding physicians, Galen.

Galen was a great anatomist and his dissections of brains provided new anatomical data which strengthened his views. He was very impressed with the size and location of the ventricles in the brain and concluded that the network of ventricles was where the 'vital spirits' or the 'animal spirits' were located. Shortly after Galen died, the Germanic invasions occurred in Western Europe leading to the loss of its knowledge of the Greek classics, which the Romans never greatly admired anyway.

In the 4th century AD, Nemesius, a bishop of Emesa in Syria, was to produce a new theory of the physical basis of mind. He claimed that he was a loyal follower of Galen but took Galen's views further. He distinguished three different mental faculties— sensation and imagination, thought and judgment, and memory— and he localised these in the different ventricles of the brain. The encephalic and cardiovascular theories, however, were not lost. Intellectual exchange, primarily in Spain, reintroduced the ideas of Aristotle and Galen to Western European thought and soon three different groups of partisans were formed supporting

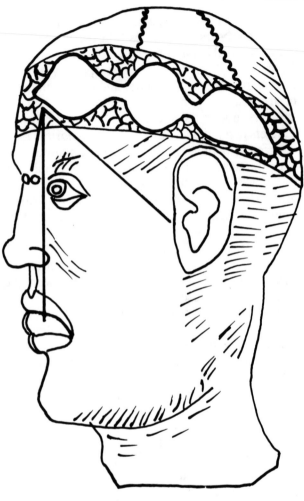

Figure 1   *Picture of Ventricular Theory*

The chambers in the brain seemed to Galen, a second century A.D. anatomist, a natural place to locate the 'animal spirit' of a living person. He located the 'natural spirit' in the liver and the 'vital spirit' in the left ventricle of the heart. Later, in the 4th century A.D., a Syrian bishop, Nemesius, extended this idea and located three different mental faculties in different ventricles of the brain. The drawing in Figure 1 is adapted from a sixteenth century account in Reisch's (1513) treatise *Margarite Philosophica*.

respectively the encephalic, cardiovascular and the ventricular theories of the mind/body relationship.

It was left to Vesalius in the early 16th century to strike the first major blow against the ventricular theory. He did this through his dissections of the human body which had previously been forbidden on theological grounds. His argument was simple: he dissected not only humans but also apes, dogs, horses, sheep and other animals and found that they *all* possessed ventricles in the brain. And yet he had been told that man was essentially different from all the animals because man possessed a soul which resided in the ventricles and all the other animals did not. At the same time the growing body of anatomical and physiological knowledge lent little support to the cardiovascular theory and Harvey's analysis of the circulation of the blood further discredited it.

Thus, by the time Shakespeare was writing his plays, there were three different theories in circulation. It is fascinating to see the way in which they are found in his writings. We are all aware that today we smuggle our views of the mind into our everyday expressions. We talk about somebody being 'switched on' or 'switched off', hinting at the computer analogy of mind. We talk about somebody being 'conditioned' to do so and so, hinting at Pavlov's physiological model of the mind. The same was true in Shakespeare's day. For example, Portia in *The Merchant of Venice* sits very delicately on the fence settling for neither the encephalic nor cardiovascular theory as she sings:

Portia: Tell me where is fancy bred,
            Or in the heart or in the head?

> Merchant of Venice,
> Act III, Scene ii

(Portia opts neither for an encephalic nor cardiovascular view.)

Or again, Sir John Falstaff in Henry IV, Part II, having just informed the chief justice that King Henry has returned in poor health from Wales, enters into a discussion as follows:

Chief Justice: I talk not of his majesty,
                      You would not come when I sent for
                      you.

Falstaff: And I hear, moreover, that his highness
                      is fallen into this same whoreson
                      apoplexy.

Chief Justice: Well, God mend him. I pray you, let me
                      speak with you.

Falstaff: This apoplexy is, as I take it, a kind
                      of lethargy, an't please your lordship;
                      a kind of sleeping in the blood, a
                      whoreson tripling.

Chief Justice: What tell me of it? Be it as it is.

Falstaff: It hath it original from much grief, from
                      study and *perturbation of the brain*. I
                      have read the causes of its effects in
                      Galen: it is a kind of deafness.

                                         Henry IV, Part II,
                                         Act IV, Scene ii
                                         (italics mine)

(Sir John takes a mixed cardiovascular and encephalic view.)

You will have noticed the references in that quotation to both
the cardiovascular ('a kind of sleeping in the blood') and encephalic ('perturbation of the brain') views. And finally, as the
following quotation shows, we find the schoolmaster Holofernes
in *Love's Labour's Lost* holding the ventricular theory mentioned
earlier.

Holofernes: This is a gift that I have, simple,
                      simple; a foolish extravagant spirit, full
                      of forms, figures, shapes, objects, ideas,
                      apprehensions, emotions, revolutions.

> *These are begot in the ventricle of*
> *memory, nourished in the womb of the*
> *pia mater*, and delivered from the
> mellowing of the occasion. But the gift
> is good in those in whom it is acute,
> and I am thankful for it.
>
> Love's Labour's Lost,
> Act IV, Scene ii
> (italics mine)
>
> *(Holofernes is a self-satisfied Nemesian.)*

All of these were written in the 1590s and Shakespeare could select his theory of mind to fit his dramatic purpose.

It is perhaps worth noting that all three plays reflected the various views in common circulation at that time. During the two centuries after Shakespeare, the ventricular and cardiovascular theories finally vanished, despite how well they seem to match one's immediate experience. They vanished because what seemed 'obvious' began to be tested against such empirical observations and results of rudimentary experiments as were gradually accumulating. Man had become a part of nature and could, as such, be subjected to increasing scientific scrutiny.

It was, as we all know, this readiness to submit ideas to observable and, ultimately, experimental facts which was one of the great advances making possible the development of science. But a radical change in 'world views' would be required before the benefits of this 'scientific' way of studying human nature could really take off. We shall return to this topic in chapters seven and eight.

Localising mind in brain

The approach of neurologists and neuropsychologists

Changing views of how mind and brain are linked

For and against localisation

Let us return for a moment to Dr Johnson and his stroke. As we indicated earlier, differing views of the mind/body relationship and the localisation of mind within the brain had been steadily accumulating support, not only from studies of man in sickness and disease, but also from the work of comparative anatomists. Such studies were to move steadily forward with the researches of people like Pierre Flourens, a French anatomist and physiologist who lived from 1794 to 1867. He made lesions in the brains of pigeons and studied the changes that occurred post-operatively in their behaviour. He concluded that there was no evidence for localisation of function within the cerebrum.

The most convincing evidence, however, was to come from careful observations of the effects of brain damage not in animals, but in humans. The possibility of demonstrating localisation of the functions of the mind in the brain took a decisive step forward on 21st February 1825 when a Frenchman, Bouillaud, read a paper to a scientific meeting in France. He

argued from his clinical studies that speech was localised in the
frontal lobes, a view already suggested by Gall. Shortly afterwards, in 1836, another Frenchman, Dax, read a paper in Mont-
pellier. He reported a series of clinical cases which he believed
demonstrated that speech disorders were linked with damage to
the left hemisphere of the brain. It was, however, not until 1865,
almost 30 years later, that Dax's manuscript was finally published by his son. In the meantime, in 1861, Paul Broca, an
anthropologist as well as a physician, heard Bouillaud's son-in-
law report a case of a patient who stopped speaking when
pressure was applied to the anterior lobes of his brain. Soon
afterwards, he himself saw a patient who had lost his speech
and could say only one word and utter oaths. The results of the
post-mortem on this patient indicated damage to the left frontal
part of the brain. It is usual to credit Paul Broca with describing
this syndrome, which consisted of an inability to speak despite
an ability to understand language in the normal way. He was
also the person who first elaborated the idea of cerebral domi-
nance of language in the left hemisphere.

The next century of thought concerning aphasia illustrated the
continuing debate about how mind is related to brain. On the
one hand, there were those who followed the lead of the early
phrenologists (those who felt the bumps on the head) and who
maintained resolutely that particular mental functions were
served by the brain's particular parts. Figure 2 is a typical
phrenologist's map showing how mental abilities and personality
traits are localised in the brain. There were, however, those who
vigorously opposed this so-called localisation view and maintained that mental ability arises from the brain's totality.

During the second half of the 20th century and especially after
the Second World War, there was a reawakening of interest in
the relationship between brain and behaviour. As sometimes
happens, it was not so much the emergence of new ideas as the
rediscovery of old ones. In this case, the views of some of the
classical neurologists, combined with new developments in measuring and understanding behaviour, gave impetus to exciting
new developments in neuropsychology.

Today there are several different approaches to the study of
brain-behaviour relationships which I shall discuss in later chap-

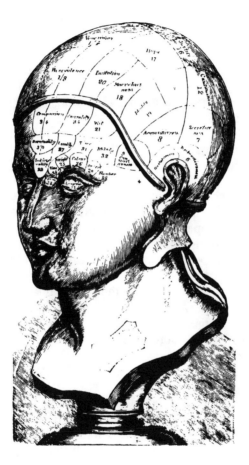

Figure 2 *A phrenologist's map*

The maps on the surface of the skull produced by phrenologists were an early example of how mental abilities (and personality characteristics) might be localised in particular parts of the brain. Some of the influential early phrenologists were not cranks but the leading anatomists of their generation.

ters. The method which has figured most prominently is a natural successor to the work of the early neurologists. It is to observe carefully the effects of damage to specific areas of the brain and, where appropriate, measure changes in mental ability and in behaviour. These techniques have also been used in studies using animals. It is noteworthy that the results of carefully controlled animal studies have been extremely important in the development of human neuropsychology. The reason is obvious. In studying patients one must, for ethical reasons, accept what comes and thus work within the limits of any brain damage, the extent of which is not precisely known. By contrast, in animal studies, the locus and extent of lesions can be much more precisely defined and aspects of the animal's behaviour before the brain damage and after it can be carefully studied and measured.

The history of studies of localisation of function illustrates well the need to be aware of the several levels (psychological, neurological, neurophysiological, biochemical) at which man may be studied. It also brings into sharp focus some contemporary and, in some people's minds, controversial issues concerning personal responsibility. For example, if my mental life and my emotions are dependent upon the proper functioning of parts or systems in my brain and if, unknown to me, something had gone wrong with them, how can I be held responsible for my thoughts, words and actions? We shall return to this later.

Changing views of localisation

The neurologist Broca gave us two important clues about localisation as he studied people like Dr Johnson whose speech had been badly impaired following a stroke. First, that the substrate for a particular behaviour may be limited to a certain part or parts of the brain. Second, that by destroying a circumscribed area you may selectively take away, temporarily or permanently, the capacity for a particular kind of behaviour. Soon after Broca's reports it became evident that strict localisation, in the terms that he suggested, had to be modified. Carl Wernicke demonstrated that there was more than one language area in the brain. And it was not even quite as simple as that. Even though an area of the brain important for language was

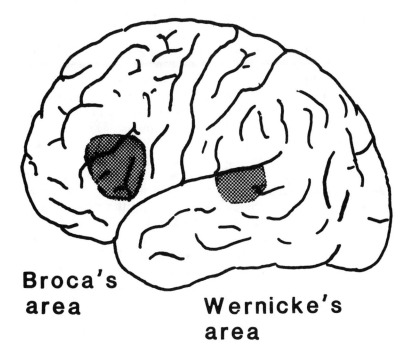

Broca's area

Wernicke's area

Figure 3 *The beginnings of localisation of function*
Neurologists' careful observations of patients with dysphasia (difficulties in producing and understanding language) following strokes began to point to circumscribed regions in the left cerebral hemisphere as the substrate for specific language abilities. Damage to Broca's area left the patient with great difficulty in producing speech; damage to Wernicke's area left the patient able to speak but unable to understand what was said.

intact, if its connections with other brain areas were damaged you might still see effects in disturbed language. In the years that followed there was a succession of reactions against what were seen as extreme localisationist positions. The distinguished British neurologist, Henry Head, was critical of what he called the 'diagram makers'. He accused them of 'lopping and twisting the symptoms' to fit the requirements of their diagrams.

With the passing of time, and especially following the Second World War, evidence accumulated to support those who argued for some degree of localisation of cerebral functions. Norman Geschwind, Professor of Neurology at Harvard until his death in 1984, wrote that the commonly held view in 1945 was that 'this type of anatomical thinking (i.e. localisation) had long since been discredited'.[1] But there were exceptions. The evidence of localisation accumulated from studies of the effects on mental life of damage to the right as well as the left hemisphere. Moreover, it was soon to be shown that in the left cerebral hemisphere one area, the planum temporale, was on average in most people one centimetre longer than on the right. This part of the brain we know on other grounds to be involved with language functions. Such observations led to renewed interest in the possibility of anatomical asymmetries in the brains, not only of humans, but also of animals. In due course, it emerged that specific morphological cerebral asymmetries are indeed evident in non-human primates and other vertebrates.[2] Did this finding, some asked, further encroach upon the uniqueness of man? Doubtless for some it did. Those who had based their belief in man's uniqueness on specific structural differences between the brains of men and animals either had to retain their beliefs by denying the truth of the anatomical findings or to move their ground to some other feature of man's physical make-up which, on present evidence, was different from animals.

These results raised intriguing questions. In humans we know that both the gross and detailed structure of the hemispheres show asymmetries which may be linked to language functions. But what do the asymmetries observed in the nonhuman primate mean? Lemay, a leading researcher in the field, recognising that all we can do at the moment is to speculate, nevertheless believes that the primate anatomical asymmetries are indeed related to asymmetrical functions. There is much, I believe, to be learned from the detailed studies of morphological asymmetries in the brains of non-human primates; much, that is, that may be of direct relevance and importance to understanding such asymmetries in humans. Neuropsychological research on monkeys and rats has already demonstrated how damage to one side of their brains had different effects on behaviour than similar damage to the other side of their brains.

Another line of evidence about cerebral asymmetries comes from studies of patients who have suffered damage either to one or other hemisphere. Such studies have shown how the consequences for mental life of damage to the left hemisphere may be different from those of damage to the right hemisphere. Further support for hemispheric differences of function comes from the study of the split-brain patients to be described later in this chapter. Those studies further underlined how the functions of the two cerebral hemispheres differ. The left hemisphere being predominantly concerned with language and motor control and the right with spatial and non-language functions (see Fig 4).

There is yet another line of evidence for us to look at. This is the result of studies of the effect of brain stimulation. In the early 1930s the Canadian neurosurgeon Wilder Penfield, in the course of surgically excising parts of the brains of epileptics, stimulated the exposed cortex and recorded the responses in the conscious patients. In this way, more direct information was available of the different functions of the two cerebral hemispheres. Such evidence gave early clues to the ways in which memories may be stored in the brain. Yet another technique which has added evidence is one in which it is possible, so to speak, to put to sleep just one cerebral hemisphere. This is done by the injection of sodium amytal into one or other carotid artery. By this means it is possible to discover something of what happens if one half of the brain is temporarily anaesthetised. This technique is frequently used before cerebral surgery in order to confirm which hemisphere is dominant for speech in a particular patient.

There are also thousands of psychological studies of normal people aimed at elucidating asymmetries in the intact brain. These are made possible by the actual wiring of the sensory

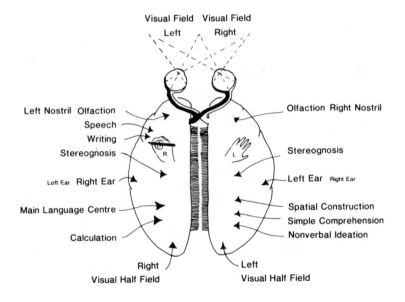

Figure 4 *The specialised functions of the cerebral hemispheres*

Results of research on patients with damage to one or other cerebral hemisphere, taken together with studies of split-brain patients and of normal
people, have converged to give a picture of how specific abilities are, in most
right-handed people, lateralised in the brain. In the drawing the corpus
callosum is shown as cut, as it is in split-brain patients.

systems from the periphery into the centre of the brain. By restricting the input briefly to one side of the visual system, for example, one can begin to study what happens when information arrives initially at one side of the brain rather than the other. One may note that when this is done the results confirm the findings of the studies of cerebral lateralisation using the methods previously mentioned.

The split brain studies

One of the most exciting approaches yet to emerge in the study of cerebral asymmetries is that associated with so-called 'split-brain' experiments. In the late 1950s, animal studies were carried out by Ronald Myers and Roger Sperry in which the fibre bundles which connect the two sides of the brain were cut (see Fig. 6). This procedure was used in humans in an attempt to limit the spread of epilepsy from one hemisphere to the other. It was carried out on a very small number of patients in California in whom epilepsy had become an intractable problem and who had not responded to other forms of therapy. In these cases, neurosurgeons cut the major fibre bundles which cross-connect the two cerebral hemispheres. These include the corpus callosum, the anterior commissure and the hippocampal commissure. Their complete sectioning is known as total commissurotomy. They discovered that after such an operation the two hemispheres seemed to behave as if they were virtually independent.

Because of the particular way in which sensory information comes into the brain's cerebral hemispheres, we know that information coming from the left hand half of the field of vision and from the left hand is routed to the right hemisphere, and vice versa for the right visual field and the right hand (see Fig. 5). From numerous studies of these so-called split brain patients it is now accepted that when the left hemisphere has access to information it can initiate speech and thus talk about the information, whereas the disconnected right hemisphere cannot. The right hemisphere apparently has good abilities to recognise things but cannot initiate speech because it cannot get access to the speech mechanisms of the left hemisphere. By presenting stimuli such as pictures or words only to the left

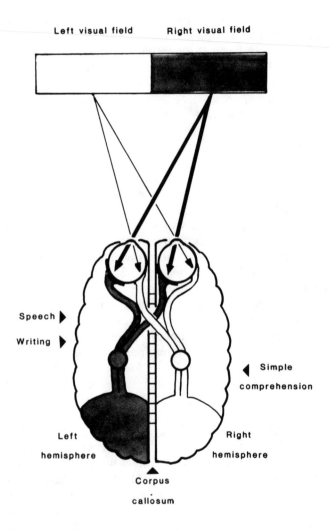

Figure 5 *The wiring of the visual system*

If someone maintains her gaze straight in front then a stimulus, say a picture
or a word, shown very briefly to the right or left of where she is facing will
go initially only to the left or right cerebral hemisphere. The data received in
the hemisphere is quickly sent to the other hemisphere across the corpus
callosum. In a split-brain patient whose corpus callosum has been cut, this
normal sharing of information is prevented.

visual field and thus to the right hemisphere or to the right visual and left hemisphere, and then asking patients to name or otherwise act upon what they have seen, it has been possible to study very carefully the particular functions of the right and left hemispheres respectively.

This kind of technique of selectively giving information to one or the other hemisphere through the eyes or ears or the sense of touch has, as mentioned above, also been applied to normal people. The results of such experiments indicate relative differences in function between the two cerebral hemispheres. These studies, combined with the studies on the surgical split brain patients and, to a lesser extent, with those on animals, particularly non-human primates, enable us to localise particular functions to the two cerebral hemispheres as illustrated in Figure 4.

Localisation and personality

So far we have concentrated on evidence for the way in which particular *mental operations* may be localised in the brain. But it is not only these which are localisable. There is evidence that quite specific emotions may be elicited by stimulating particular parts of the brain. Such evidence comes primarily from experimental work on animals. In the human domain the most dramatic demonstrations have come from the study of patients who have a particular form of epilepsy originating in the temporal lobes. In some of those patients personality changes have been observed associated with loss of interest in their sex life. This decrease in libidinal interest is, however, often paralleled by an increase in social aggressiveness. The report of one such study claims that patients also show one or more characteristic personality trait. The list includes: (1) laboured and intense emotional reactions; (2) an increase in religious interest, occasionally manifested as an ardent religious conversion; (3) a tendency to keep extensive diaries and autobiographical notes; (4) a deep pervasive moralistic feeling sometimes coupled with paranoia and; (5) a notable lack of humour.

It has also been claimed that these traits are correlated with lateralisation. The patients who had epilepsy from a right temporal lobe focus displayed excessive emotional tendencies. In contrast, those who have left temporal lobe epilepsy had a

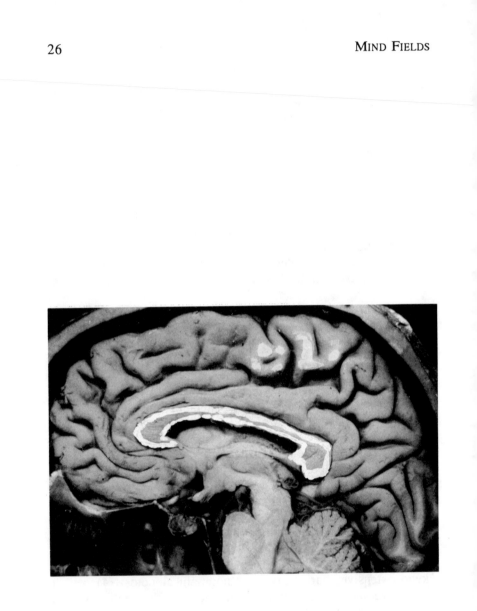

Figure 6 *The corpus callosum connecting the two cerebral hemispheres*

The photograph shows the inside wall of the right hemisphere of a human brain. The area highlighted in white is the corpus callosum made up of some 200 million nerve fibres which cross connect the two cerebral hemispheres.

tendency to moral self-scrutiny and towards extensive philosophical explanations. Apparently, patients with epileptic foci outside the temporal lobes do not normally present with abnormalities of emotion and behaviour. One aspect of this list of personality traits of epileptics, namely an increase in religious interest, has been made the basis for a whole theory of the neuropsychology of religious conversion!

Recent developments in brain imaging

Several exciting developments have taken place in the past decade in the methods used to visualise the brain, its structure and activity. These methods do not involve lesioning the brain nor probing it in any way. The method which is giving some of the most dramatic results and which is being used by psychologists working with neurologists and neurosurgeons is Positron Emission Tomography or PET scan for short. Through this technique it is possible to detect the activity of different areas of the brain by measuring their relative consumption of a temporarily radioactive form of the brain's normal fuel, glucose. The more active the neurones in a particular area of the brain, the more glucose they burn up. Using this technique, researchers have identified particular areas of the brain as being relatively more active when a person is, for example, listening to music or reading or just daydreaming. As an example, consider one such set of studies reported by Michael Posner and his colleagues in the journal *Science* in 1988 in which they showed how the human brain localises mental operations of the kind suggested by cognitive psychologists.[3] They studied how, when normal people are reading a single word, there are average changes in cerebral blood flow in localised brain areas during 40 seconds of such cognitive activity. They concluded from their studies that they provide strong support for the localisation of mental operations when performing such tasks.

What is lateralised?

All of this is very interesting, but it does not of itself answer the question of what it is that is lateralised or localised to one side of the brain or the other. To summarise, we now know that the left hemisphere is better at dealing with letters and words, or language-related sounds, at coping with the control of complex voluntary movement, at retaining verbal material in memory, at looking after speech, reading, writing and arithmetic. By contrast, the right hemisphere is better at handling complex geometrical patterns, is better at handling the perception and storage of faces, is better at handling music, is better at handling the tactile interpretation of complex patterns and is better at guiding one's movements in space. All this, then, we already know about localisation of function. But the question remains: what is it that is lateralised? Are there any fundamental differences between the two cerebral hemispheres in the way they handle information coming in to them or initiate processes and bodily movements? If so, what are they? A number of views have been put forward.

One early proposal, put forward by Josephine Semmes, arose out of her studies of World War II veterans suffering from brain injuries. She argued that, whereas the right hemisphere has its functions distributed in a diffuse manner, the left hemisphere has its functions collected in a very focalised way. From Josephine Semmes' early ideas other researchers argued that the hemispheres use two distinct modes of processing incoming information. Note here that *we move from a level of analysis of asymmetry in terms of neuroanatomical centres to a description of psychological modes of processing information.* According to this view, the left hemisphere operates in a more logical, analytical, computer-like fashion. The right hemisphere is more concerned with getting the overall impression of a stimulus input and organising the information in terms of wholes. This approach, of course, is entirely an inference from the data. Yet another way of distinguishing between the hemispheres has been suggested by Doreen Kimura. In her view, the left hemisphere deals with verbal functions but is not specialised just for verbal function but rather for motor functions of all kinds of which speech production is but one example.

It is evident from this brief consideration of a perennial problem in neuropsychology, namely localisation of function, that we need several different levels at which to investigate the problems if we are to begin to do justice to the complexity of the issues that we face. It is evident also that we cannot adequately handle the issue if we investigate it only at the level of the neurophysiology of single neurones or neuronal interactions. Any comprehensive analysis must take into account other levels, such as the biochemical and psychological.

Granted then that neuroanatomical, neurophysiological and neuropsychological studies all support the conclusion that the two cerebral hemispheres are not identical either in structure or function, a further issue arises. Are the differences in cognitive abilities between people evident in everyday activities—things like high versus low intelligence, being better at music than at mathematics, better at art than English—simply reflecting differences in brain architecture? This is certainly one of the most challenging and elusive goals of contemporary neuropsychology.

Those who work in the field argue that there are a number of reasons to expect that variations in normal brain organisation may contribute to individual differences in psychological abilities. For example, there is considerable evidence for moderate heritability of particular cognitive abilities. It is logical to suppose that some of this heritable variation may be due to genetically determined variation in neurological structure. For example, identical twins score as similarly on intelligence tests as the same person tested twice, a finding not much affected by the twins being reared separately.

It is becoming increasingly apparent that there may also be variations in brain anatomy related to gender. These differences are large enough that it would be very surprising if they did not have consequences for cognitive abilities. There are, in fact, reliable cognitive and other differences evident between the sexes. When considering such gender differences, we need always to remember that any average differences between groups of males and groups of females may tell us little about any particular male or female.

Where group mean differences have been found, the variations among women and among men may far exceed those between the average man and the average woman. Having said that, we can note three gender differences that seem actually to exist. First, men behave more aggressively than women. This applies whether we look at laboratory studies or statistics of the commitment of violent crimes. It seems that the male hormone testosterone may be partly responsible, though it doubtless also has several roots. Second, in virtually every society men are socially dominant. Third, on spatial tasks men tend to surpass women. By spatial tasks we mean such things as vertically rotating an object to match its orientation against a standard object, of finding one's way around an unfamiliar town, or doing geometry problems.

It looks increasingly likely then that some, at least, of the observed cognitive differences between individuals may be due to differences in brain organisation and not simply due to differential histories of socialisation. It is plausible, for example, to interpret some cognitive differences between the sexes as at least partly due to neurological factors. It is also likely that cognitive abilities of the same individual at different times vary according to changes in brain chemistry. As Doreen Kimura has expressed it recently, 'Some of the observed male-female differences in cognitive ability appear to be determined by sex hormones working on brain systems.' She has recently examined the possibility that fluctuations in hormones *within* an individual might also be reflected in cognitive changes. Together with her student, Elizabeth Hampson, she administered an extensive battery of cognitive and motor tests to normally cycling women at two phases of the menstrual cycle in order to detect any hormone-mediated changes in performance. The women showed changes across the menstrual cycle on speeded articulation and manual skills and on some non-verbal/social tests. Doreen Kimura points out that the fluctuations in abilities one has observed are not large and that for most women hormone fluctuations do not affect everyday life.[4] An important point which we take up and consider in more detail in the next chapter.

Converging approaches to localisation—an illustrative example from an everyday activity

What's in a face?

'The nose of Cleopatra: had it been shorter, the whole (face of the) earth would have changed.' This famous aphorism of Pascal, all the more memorable for the pun that it contains, says as much about history in general as it does about faces. You could argue, I suppose, that a shorter nose would not only have *de-faced* the beauty of Cleopatra, but it would also have changed the *political face* of the world. Perhaps Antony would not have fallen in love with this last Queen of Egypt; perhaps his conflict with Caesar would have taken a different turn; perhaps the history of the Roman Empire, and consequently that of Western Europe, might have taken a quite different course. But we cannot go on with our perhapses. It at least gives me a chance to introduce the fascinating question of what's in a face?

When the first postage stamps were introduced in 1840, they had on them the features of Queen Victoria. The assumption which the early postage stamp designers followed was that we have an ability to discriminate and retain information about faces which probably represents the ultimate in so-called non-verbal perceptual skills and thus the possibility of effective forgery of the new stamps was minimal. It seems that not only can we distinguish among an infinity of faces, but we are also relatively good at recognising large numbers of strangers' faces when we have only seen them briefly on one occasion. Familiar faces, it seems, can be quite reliably identified even if only a very small fragment is seen, or the whole face is seen under very poor viewing conditions.

Dr Samuel Johnson's traumatic experience of losing his ability to speak because of localised damage to his brain is paralleled in other people who seem to lose the very specific ability to recognise hitherto familiar faces. Several such cases have been documented. Figure 7 shows a brain scan of a patient who, following brain damage, found himself unable to recognise faces. As the figure caption explains, there is localised damage mostly to the right posterior part of the brain—a common finding with such patients. It was not that his visual perception generally was impaired. He could recognise houses, birds, cows, motor cars, cups, saucers, but not faces. It seemed that the inability to recognise faces was very specific and followed damage to the posterior occipital lobes of the brain and frequently on the right side. Perhaps, even more surprising, were published reports of patients whose difficulty was that they could no longer recognise other specific perceptual categories; in one case birds, in another case cows.

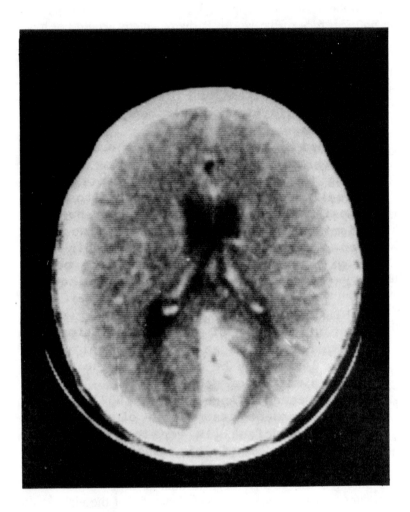

Figure 7   *Brain scan of a prosopagnosic patient.*
The figure shows a CT scan of a patient suffering from prosopagnosia, the inability to recognise faces: note a lighter area to the right of the midline at the bottom of the scan, indicating damage to the area of the brain believed to be specially involved in face processing.

There is, for example, a case in the literature describing a farmer who became unable to identify one cow from another having previously been able to recognise them individually. A similar case has been described of a very competent ornithologist, who seemed to know the name of every bird, but following the onset of his illness was no longer able to give the name to any bird, even though he would have done it promptly before the onset of his illness. Detailed studies of cases such as these have now helped us to identify those parts of the brain which need to be intact if this ability to recognise faces is to continue normally.

There is a good deal of evidence that the damage to the brain producing this result is highly localised and some, though not all, investigators believe that it indicates that it is more likely to be in the right than in the left side of the brain. But then one may go on to ask, 'It's all very well to say it's localised in a particular part of the brain, but how are the cells in those brain areas organised for carrying out the task of face recognition?' There is now some very exciting evidence from recording from single cells in the brains of alert monkeys to show that particular cells or columns of cells are dedicated to dealing with face recognition. What is perhaps even more exciting and surprising is that certain columns of cells deal with the processing of the full face appearance and others with different profile views. Yet other columns of cells, it seems, may be earmarked for the processing of emotional expression in faces.

So not only have neuropsychologists studied face perception at the level of single cells and columns of cells—a very 'bottom-up' or reductionist approach—they have also worked at the level of systems or areas of the brain specially dedicated to face processing—a 'higher level' according to Churchland and Sejnowski's level of organisation approach.[5] But there is more. There are also the cognitive psychologists who have modelled the face recognition processes in terms of modules and dual processing routes. Figure 8 illustrates one such model currently enjoying support amongst cognitive psychologists. The model has been built to account for results from studies of face perception in normal people and from case studies of patients with brain damage producing very selective difficulties in face perception.

When we see the face of someone whom we know we draw on all sorts of information stored in the brain as we seek to remember their name. 'She goes to the same church as me', 'She's an Australian', 'She's a keen tennis player', and so on. But how is this achieved? Only relatively recently have cognitive psychologists made a sustained effort to answer this deceptively simple question. The theoretical models they build attempt to explain how people access the relevant semantic information and names from familiar faces. Figure 8 is typical of such models. It assumes that when a familiar face is identified a recognition unit (nothing necessarily to do with brain cells; simply a hypothetical component of the model) responds to the surface form of the face and signals that it looks familiar. Subsequently, so-called identity-specific semantic codes and name codes are accessed in sequence. The model further assumes that expression codes and visually-observed semantic codes are formed independently from the part of the system that determines the face's identity. The authors claim that the results of studies of brain damaged people who find it difficult to recognise familiar faces, as well as studies of normal people, fit this model. Moreover, they believe it helps to account for a number of the findings such as that everyday slips in recognition often take the form of an apparent 'block' in proceeding from one part of the sequence to another, as when people can classify faces as familiar more quickly than they can classify them by occupation. What is important for our present discussion is that this model, and others like it, make no reference to brain cells, but are valid, useful and important models of the processes of face recognition and have led to studies that have produced data that any adequate account of face recognition will need to explain. Localisation in this context would mean that different aspects of the overall process of face recognition can be located in hypothetical modules which process the information that arrives when we see a familiar face. The extent to which the modules in such information flow charts correspond to the activities of aggregations of cells in the brain is a topic of lively contemporary research in neuropsychology. The models are important in guiding the direction of such research and of generating hypotheses.

The analyses of face perception at different levels in psycho-

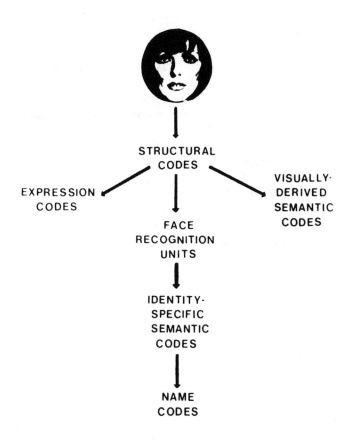

Figure 8 *A typical cognitive psychologist's model of face perception*

The sensory input received when a familiar face is seen is presumed to pass through a series of modules each of which provides a different type of additional information culminating in the recognition process.

logy and neuroscience thus supplement and complement one
another. The excitement of cognitive neuroscience, which we
discuss in more detail in chapter four, is that it promises to
provide ways of bridging the gulf between the single cell recording approaches and the cognitive modelling approaches.

**How the empirical approach corrects extreme and simplistic
localisationist views**
It would be easy to overstate the case for localisation of function.
For example, the work described above based on recordings
from single cells of the alert monkey's brain certainly indicates
a very specific kind of localisation. However, these same workers have more recently studied other cells in the same region of
the brain which fire if appropriate stimuli are presented to the
monkey but which remain silent if the animal itself produces the
same stimulus. For example, if a monkey itself makes a characteristic cry, such an auditory stimulus does not make cells fire,
but if these cries are recorded and played back then a marked
cellular response occurs in the self-same cells. The same occurs
in the visual modality.

In similar vein, others have raised the same issue. Thus, Dr
Micky Goldberg and his colleagues pose the question: 'Are there
pitfalls in recording from single or multiple units?' Their reply
is '. . .a given correlation of single neuron activity with a certain
input or output measure may not tell us how the neuron is
involved in the analysis of the input or in production of that
output. This can occur because the operation of the network may
be determined more by the pattern of cell connectives than by
the discharge patterns or properties of individual neurons.' And
they point out the converse also applies when they say, 'It may
be equally misleading to ignore the biophysical properties of
individual neurons and only study their information processing
potential as units within a network.'[6]

A similar point can be made from the results of neuropsychological studies of memory. Thus, Professor Mortimer
Mishkin and Dr Tim Appenzeller in their 1987 *Scientific American* article, 'The Anatomy of Memory', summarise the many
and varied sites in the brain which have been associated with
memory and learning.[6] Mortimer Mishkin and Tim Appenzeller

summarised the results of twenty years research aimed at identifying neural structures and stations (large arrays of cells) that contribute to memory. Figure 9 adapted from their paper illustrates how memory loss in human beings may not be caused by damage or disease exclusively confined to one brain location. Rather, in so far as there is localisation of memory, it is distributed over several interconnected sites.

Later in the same paper, Mishkin and Appenzeller point out that in addition to memory there may be a second system of learning which they call 'habit'. This is founded not on knowledge or even on memories but on automatic connections between stimulus and response. Defined in this way, habits are reminiscent of the automatic stimulus-response linkages which the behaviourist psychologists argued were the basis of all learning.

The point of interest for us is that the behaviourist would have excluded all such terms as 'mind' and 'knowledge'. As such, behaviourism stood in opposition to cognitive psychology, so dominant today, and which relies on these concepts to account for much of behaviour. But the possibility, raised by the work of Mishkin and many others, that learning is built on two quite different systems, non-cognitive habits and cognitive memories, offers a way of reconciling the behaviourist and cognitive approaches. As Mishkin and Appenzeller put it: 'If neural mechanisms for both kinds of learning do exist, behaviour could be a blend of automatic responses to stimuli and actions guided by knowledge and expectations.' Or, following the terminology favoured here, a combination of the bottom-up and top-down approaches; both are important and once again mind matters.

Thus whilst there is clearly need for caution in interpreting the results of neurophysiological and neuropsychological studies of localisation of cognitive functions, that does not mean we can deny the weight of evidence pointing to the tightness of the link between mind and brain. Rather, it means that we have a lot more work to do in spelling out the nature of that link. For our present discussion, the point remains that there is a very tight link between mental events and the physical embodiment of those events in the brain.

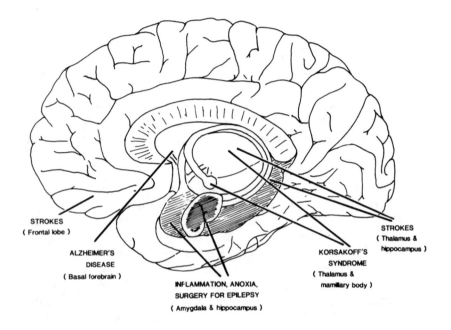

STROKES
(Frontal lobe)

ALZHEIMER'S
DISEASE
(Basal forebrain)

INFLAMMATION, ANOXIA,
SURGERY FOR EPILEPSY
(Amygdala & hippocampus)

KORSAKOFF'S
SYNDROME
(Thalamus &
mamillary body)

STROKES
(Thalamus &
hippocampus)

Figure 9 *Distributed localisation of memory*

The drawing of a cut-away of a human brain illustrates the variety of sites which, when damaged by disease and other events, can result in memory loss. The concept of localisation when applied to a cognitive function such as memory cannot therefore be validly applied in a simplistic fashion which suggests that there is just one localised site. Rather the empirical data point towards distributed interacting circuits.

Damaged brains and disordered minds

Maintaining a balance

In sketching out his overview of changing fashions in psychiatry, Lipowski commented, 'Another current fad is to tell patients that they suffer from a chemical imbalance in the brain.' 'The explanatory power of this statement,' he went on, 'is of the same order as if you said to the patient, "You're alive!".' But such statements are common and serve to confuse etiology with correlation and cause with mechanism. It can so easily give a patient the impression that the chemical imbalance (if so there be) is the *only* cause of her illness and that personal efforts and responsibilities have no part to play in getting better. Lipowski sums it up well, 'To assume, as we all do, that biochemical processes underlie mental activity and behaviour *does not imply that they are the causal agents but rather mediating mechanisms*' (italics mine).[1] It is in this context that we now consider, by way of illustration, some of the areas of neuroscience where research is currently intense.

Neural tissue transplantation

In Chapter 1 I mentioned a media report that Mohammed Ali was considering a brain transplant. We now pick up again the issue of neural tissue transplantation. Attempts to transplant nervous tissue are not new. There are records of neural transplants being tried around the turn of the century. However, the restricted techniques available at that time made it unlikely that any degree of success would be achieved. As early as 1914, the first attempt to transplant nervous tissue from a foetus had been reported and it was noted that the graft had survived a short while and it was argued that it had, to some extent, been incorporated into the circuitry of the host brain. The early work tended to concentrate on studies using amphibians and chicks. The modern phase of neural transplantation began in 1971 when two groups of workers produced evidence indicating that transplanting parts of the brains of embryos, which were rich in a neurotransmitter called dopamine, held out hope of success. Since that time there have been many studies which lend increasing support to the belief that tissue that has been grafted can begin to re-establish some of the damaged neuronal circuitry of the host brain. Most of the experimental work has been done on rats. Tissue from the central nervous system, if it is to be transplanted successfully, requires an embryonic donor and requires that the transplantation be done at a very specific development stage.

The tissue may be transplanted in a number of different ways. One technique is to take a solid piece of tissue from the embryo and place it directly into a ventricle (a natural cavity in a brain) of the host animal. Another is to take out a piece of the brain of the host animal and to actually transplant a piece of the embryonic neural tissue into the cavity that has been formed. A third technique has been used by the Swedish workers active in this field; their method is based on standard cell culturing techniques. The tissue to be grafted is put into suspension and this is then injected into the host brain (see Fig. 10).

The pace of research on this topic is accelerating. A recent report given at the 1990 meeting of the American Association for the Advancement of Science indicates just how fast things are moving. Professor George Allen described, for example, how remarkable progress was made by a 40-year-old woman given a brain implant to treat Parkinson's disease. Not all patients respond so well but the successes so far achieved have encouraged Professor Allen and his co-workers to perform more implant operations than anywhere else in the world. It may not be necessary to use foetal tissue for implantation. Professor Fred Gage at the University of California in San Diego has experimented with genetically engineered cells, grown in the laboratory, which can be designed to produce the missing chemical messenger. So far the work is with animals and several years away from any realistic attempt at human implantation. Many questions remain unanswered such as whether the effects of the tissue transplant are diffuse, or whether they are very specific. On balance, the evidence points to the effects being due to continuous neurotransmitter release by the transplanted tissue rather than by any specific re-innervation of damaged pathways. The possible relevance of this to human neurological conditions focuses on alleviating the symptoms of Parkinson's Disease. Since most of the studies have been concerned with transplanting tissue which releases dopamine and since post-mortem studies of Parkinson's patients' brains have shown a significant depletion of dopamine, it seemed an 'obvious' next step to contemplate the possibility of using tissue transplants to alleviate some of the symptoms of Parkinson's Disease.

In 1982, a report was published of an attempt to transplant tissue from the adrenal cortex of a Parkinson's patient, and grafting it into an area of the patient's brain known as the caudate nucleus. The patient was severely afflicted by Parkinson's Disease, and the report at that time indicated only a slight improvement following neural transplantation. There seems little doubt that this field of investigation will accelerate and we may expect some exciting developments in the years ahead. In the meantime, there is all the difference between the journalistic description of this work as 'brain transplants' and the very modest and conservative descriptions by those working in the field who describe their work simply as attempted neural tissue transplantation.

At an April 1991 workshop of the European Brain and Behaviour Society on recovery of function following brain damage, Professor A Björklund, one of the pioneers of research in this field, reviewed the work on neural transplants and recovery of function in animals. Focusing on the mechanisms of transplant-

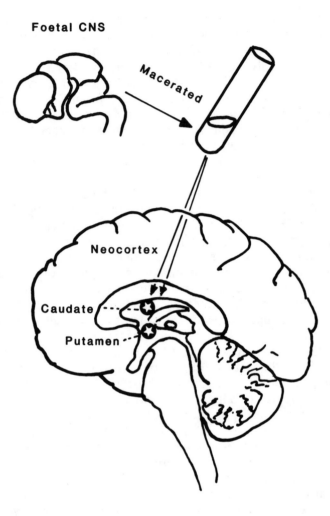

Foetal CNS

Figure 10 *Neural tissue implants*

Foetal tissue from the developing central nervous system is prepared in
solution and injected into the caudate and putamen of a patient's brain through
a hole in the skull. Using this and similar techniques several hundred patients
worldwide have undergone treatment for Parkinson's disease. Clearly there
are serious ethical issues to be addressed in the use of foetal tissue and already
work is in hand to generate genetically engineered cells grown in the laboratory.

induced recovery of function in the subcortically denervated hippocampus, he indicated that such implants have been shown to ameliorate learning and memory impairments. As regards the human studies, Professor E Hitchcock, reviewing his own and other people's work, was cautiously optimistic. He believed that 'future applications and developments in the extending of the treatment to other neuro-degenerative diseases and the use of cultured cells or growth factors are likely to establish neural transplantation as a viable treatment modality'.

Schizophrenia

There are still parts of the world where the hearing of voices and the firm conviction that one possesses extraordinary gifts, mental powers and insights denied to others, can lead to privileges and, in places, the ascription of divine possession. The experiences which are subjectively felt during an acute attack of schizophrenia may, at times, not be unlike what I have just described, but they may also be terrifying and overwhelming.

Schizophrenia, whilst not an uncommon problem, remains one of today's major medical puzzles. We now know, for example, that its onset occurs most frequently in young people during adolescence, and in the 20s and early 30s. It is significant that over half the population of the large psychiatric hospitals at their peak occupancy in 1954 consisted of people diagnosed as schizophrenic. Many of them had been resident for more than two years, and most were likely to end their days in hospital. Today we remember, with thankfulness, how the situation changed radically, due largely to the application of methods of clinical care underpinned by the fortuitous discovery of medications which, although still only partially effective, suppress the most acute and distressing symptoms.

During the past twenty years, there has been no one dramatic scientific breakthrough in this field such as has revolutionised our understanding of some other diseases. There has nevertheless been a steady accumulation of psychosocial and biological information about this distressing condition. As we noted in an earlier chapter, one of the most exciting recent developments has been the possibility of actually visualising the activity and structure of the brain without any harm to the person concerned. This is made possible by new techniques of visual imaging of the brain. There is great excitement today that this may at last lead to rapid progress towards understanding something of the nature and causes and then to the most suitable means of treating or even preventing schizophrenia. Figure 11 portrays the different levels of activity in specific regions in the brain of a schizophrenic patient using the technique of Positron Emission Tomography (PET Scan). However, as a 1990 study published in the *British Journal of Psychiatry* makes clear, not all investigators have found this so-called hypofrontality in schizophrenia.

Several levels of investigation are needed
The study of schizophrenia provides another example of why we need to take account of several different levels of investigation. At one level it is clear that what precipitates the onset of an attack of schizophrenia may be something of a psychosocial nature. It has been observed, for example, that patients after years without positive symptoms, may relapse if they are exposed to unrealistic expectations of social performance whilst they are undergoing rehabilitation, only to show rapid recovery when they return to sheltered conditions. Clearly the social environment is an important modulating factor. Or again, in psychiatric research, there has, in recent years, been an emphasis on the effects of so-called 'life events' in causing the onset of schizophrenia, depression and other illnesses. Acute life events, not necessarily stressful, have been shown to precede the onset of schizophrenia. Studies of the types of psychosocial factors which may precipitate the onset of schizophrenia help to build up more general and useful theories of the effects of environmental influences on behaviour and mental life. It is clear that how the caring staff and the local community behave affects the management of schizophrenic symptoms. Moving from a secluded hospital to community-based services may have profound effects on the health of schizophrenics. The psychosocial level of study of schizophrenia then remains essential.

As we noted earlier, effective alleviation of the more distressing symptoms of schizophrenia has been available now for over thirty years. The initial prototypical drug was chlorpromazine and was introduced by accident. Its successors have all emerged

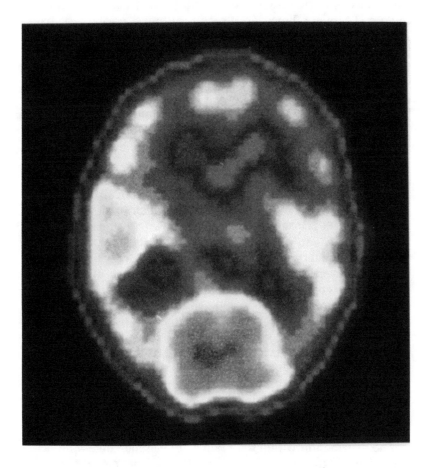

Figure 11 *A schizophrenic's brain*

Using the technique of Positron Emission Tomography (PET Scan) it is possible to assess the relative levels of metabolic activity in different parts of the brain. In the figure it is apparent that there are abnormally low levels of activity in the frontal lobes as shown in this black and white reproduction by more dark areas at the top of the picture (the front of the brain).

out of empirical evidence rather than any clear-cut theory. These drugs, the so-called neuroleptics, are effective in treating the symptoms of acute episodes of the illness and may also prevent relapse. There are, however, it seems, at times, prices to be paid for such medication notwithstanding all their beneficial effects. There may be neurological side effects, such as slowly developing difficulties in moving one's limbs accurately. Such problems seem to develop when some neuroleptic drugs are taken over extended periods. Moreover, and particularly worrying, such consequences seem at times to be irreversible. The drive is on, however, to discover new drugs that combine greater efficiency in dealing with the symptoms whilst producing few unwanted side effects.

The effectiveness of some drugs in the relief of schizophrenic symptoms accelerated the search for a biochemical basis of the disease. There are neurones in the brain which function because they contain a transmitter substance known as dopamine. It is found that all the drugs so far known to be effective in the treatment of schizophrenia antagonise (oppose the action of) dopamine, even though they may differ from one another with respect to a number of other pharmacological actions. For this reason, dopamine receptor antagonism is currently a strong candidate as a possible mechanism of the anti-psychotic effects of these drugs. A second reason for interest in the dopamine mechanism is that other drugs, the amphetamines, can in certain instances actually induce schizophrenia-like symptoms. They exert at least some of their effects in the brain by enhancing rather than antagonising dopamine release. It is for this reason that the front-runner among theories of schizophrenia's chemical basis is the so-called dopamine hypothesis.

The distribution within the brain of dopamine-containing neurones is now known in considerable detail. This means that it is possible to focus research attention on those parts of the brain which show a concentration of dopamine-containing neurones and so to speculate as to their specific involvement in schizophrenia. Neuropathological studies of the brain begin to clarify this issue. They have shown that there are structural changes in the brains of some schizophrenics specifically in the temporal lobes.

What is of particular interest is that there seems to be an asymmetry about the schizophrenic's brain; the structural changes in question are usually more marked in the left hemisphere than in the right. In addition, studies of the brains of chronic schizophrenics using recent brain scanning techniques show specific localised changes. It seems that these changes cannot be attributed simply to the physical treatments given to the patients. In cases where there has been early onset of the disease there is evidence that the posterior part of the left hemisphere of the brain is less well developed. This may have aetiological significance. The significance of such structural changes in the brain has been clarified by means of post-mortem studies. When compared with patients with disorders like depression, the brains of patients with schizophrenia were 5 to 6% lighter and had a 90% increase in cross sectional area of the temporal horn of the lateral ventricles. Researchers suggest that such findings *may* indicate that the site of the pathology of schizophrenia is the temporal lobe.

There is yet another level at which schizophrenia may be investigated. This arises from an interest in possible genetic factors contributing to schizophrenia. Schizophrenic illnesses are more commonly seen amongst first-degree relatives of patients with schizophrenia than amongst the relatives of patients with non-psychiatric illnesses. Schizophrenia is more frequent in the adopted children of schizophrenic mothers than in other adoptees. In twins, when one member of a pair suffers from schizophrenia, the other is two or three times as likely to do so when the twins are identical. Schizophrenia, however, is not a simple genetic condition. Only a minority, about 20%, of patients showing the disease have a relative who suffers from an unequivocal schizophrenic illness. Despite these findings, caution is required before jumping too readily to conclusions about the importance of the genetic factor. There is little support for a single gene as the sole source of resemblance between relatives. What is a promising alternative is the so-called liability threshold. If it is assumed that the risk of developing schizophrenia is regarded as continually distributed in the population, then only individuals whose liability exceeds a given threshold will actually manifest the disorder.

For our present purposes, the lesson to be derived from this brief consideration of schizophrenia is *that mental life and its biological substrates are inextricably interwoven.* How they are interwoven is dependent upon the social context and the physical environment. The psychophysical unity of man is thus emphasised. It is also evident, yet again, that there are several different levels at which we can study man and his behaviour. In considering schizophrenia we have noted the pharmacological, the psychosocial and the genetic levels. We might have added there is recent evidence gathered in different parts of the world which points to an excess of winter births associated with the incidence of schizophrenia. This excess, though small, can hardly be a matter of chance. It thus gives rise to theories of causation which involve the possibility of a viral infection. In this sense the study of man and disease, as far as schizophrenia is concerned, moves to yet another level, the molecular.

Dementia in old age
Changes in mental life and emotional experiences are, fortunately, not always as distressing as those we see in schizophrenia. Nevertheless, even less disabling changes such as occur as we all get old may be related to identifiable changes in brain anatomy or biochemistry. The link between the mental and physical may be more subtle but just as real if only we could pin it down. And if we can pin it down, then given time, we may be able to do something about it. Let us take ageing as a further example of the tightening of the mind/brain link.

Emphases certainly change. Twenty years ago we were living in a decade of anxiety, ten years ago it was depression, today it seems we are entering the age of dementia. Certainly the incidence and prevalence of Alzheimer's disease and of the AIDS dementia complex grow. Once again these are age old problems given a new twist and a new urgency. It seems that the poet Juvenal in the second century AD was poignantly aware of some of the devastating features of dementia. He wrote, 'Worse by far than any bodily hurt is dementia: for he who has it no longer knows the names of his slaves or recognises the friend with whom he has dined the night before, or those whom he had begotten and bought up.'[2] Although in the past decade research on Alzheimer's disease has mushroomed, as yet no cure is in sight, but it is to neuroscientists that we look for help.

Cognitive gerontology—lessons for us all

We have known for many years that the proportion of elderly people in the population will continue to rise steadily. There are large increases in those aged more than 75, who show a high prevalence of chronic disorders, and this results amongst other things in significant costs for adequate medical care. The urgency of the need to understand more about age-related diseases and the ageing process is ever more apparent. Already a new specialisation has emerged known as *cognitive gerontology*. This may be defined as the attempt to discover what mental changes occur in the elderly, when they begin to occur, how fast the changes take place and whether there is anything that we can usefully do about them. One of the great problems has been to discover whether there is any single measurement which can capture all the cognitive changes that occur or whether we need a wide variety of different measures in order to track the different changes that occur in ageing.

One of the most important age-related disorders is dementia. Many studies have been undertaken of its prevalence in the community. Typically it occurs in about 5% of the population over the age of 65. Almost all the studies agree that there is a considerable rise in the prevalence of dementia over the age of 75, with an incidence of something like 20% over 80 years of age. Dementia, however, is not a simple category. There are different types. Senile dementia of the Alzheimer's type and that resulting from several small strokes (labelled multi-infarct) are thought to account between them for more than 90% of the dementias seen in the community. Only 8–12% of cases referred to a hospital for the investigation of dementia are diagnosed as multi-infarct dementia, the majority being diagnosed as senile dementia of the Alzheimer's type. Post-mortem series have found somewhat different proportions with 50% of the Alzheimer's type, 20% of the multi-infarct type and 20% showing a combination of both pathologies.

As research into cognitive changes in old age has increased, it has become clear that poor performance is not the same as demonstration of cognitive decline. Many other conditions can lead to reduced cognitive performance, such as poor education, low IQ or just illness, and these must be distinguished from progressive decline which results from ageing. The existing longitudinal data suggest that by a given age only a proportion of individuals have declined in cognitive function and this proportion increases with advancing age. One report indicates that between the ages of 74 and 81 almost half the population showed cognitive decline.

It is not only neurological and metabolic disorders which can produce dementia in ageing. Other chronic conditions prevalent in the elderly are also likely to impair cognitive functioning. Some relationships, indeed, have already been clearly established. For example, performance on IQ and memory tests declined over a 10 year period in hypertensive elderly people but not those who were normally tensive. Again, cardiovascular disease is associated with decline in cognitive function as is chronic obstructive lung disease.

Investigation has also been carried out by looking at the actual pathological histological changes that are evident in the brains of those who suffer from senile dementia of the Alzheimer's type. The changes found in the brains of such patients are also found, but to a lesser extent, in the brains of apparently normal, ageing subjects. In other words, most of the other changes found in the abnormal brains are quantitative rather than qualitative. It is still not clear whether senile dementia of the Alzheimer's type is a distinct entity or an extreme manifestation of normal ageing. The point here is a simple one. Investigation to understand what is happening in ageing needs to go on at all these different levels. The psychosocial, the cognitive, the neuronal and the biochemical.

The supergeriatrics
One of the leading research groups in the field in the United Kingdom is directed by Professor Patrick Rabbit. He has pointed out that as well as wanting to understand the particular changes that occur in ageing in cognitive performance, we also need to know why it is that certain aged people perform better than the normal for their age. Why are they so lucky? Why do these

supergeriatrics manage to perform as well as they do? It is important to know this because by knowing something about their background, we may be able to increase the numbers of such geriatrics.

In reviewing his work recently, Professor Rabbit looked ahead to the next steps in investigation in this field. He pointed out that the time has now arrived when different pathologies which occur in old age may be shown to produce differing rates of cognitive change. Thus the question of the epidemiology of cognitive changes in old age is both a pressing issue and one which may now be addressed. Equally important, and one which is a good example of what we are wanting to address in this book, is the need to take account of the effects of life circumstances and of social factors and see how these affect the rate of cognitive change in old age. It is clear that the extent to which social support systems are effective may well mitigate the effects of age. And in turn, the effects to which social planning can mitigate the rate of cognitive change in old age is an issue worthy of urgent and serious consideration. Long term practical aims of such lines of research are to determine the factors which progressively put elderly people at risk when they try to lead independent lives in the community. If such factors are better understood and are considered in time, they may well allow us to avert some of the catastrophes in which the lives of many elderly people prematurely end.

Once again, then, we have looked at a particular issue which involves both the neuroscientist and the psychologist. We have seen that in order to begin to do justice to the issues that we face with all their complexity, we must be ready to investigate at several complementary levels. In this case we need to look at the brain pathology involved, we need to look at possible changes in brain chemistry, we need to look at the specific changes in mental or cognitive abilities which occur and we need to look at the effects of the social circumstances surrounding the elderly and the extent to which modifying these would mitigate the worst effects of the ageing process.

Taking stock
Our focus of interest has been how an individual's mental and

emotional life may reflect the efficiency of the functioning of his brain. To illustrate the point we have considered evidence for localisation of function in the brain, dementia, schizophrenia, and cognitive changes that take place with normal ageing. In each case we have been forcefully reminded of the tightening of the mind/brain link.

In our discussion of cerebral localisation, we noted that evidence of an anatomical and behavioural kind is already emerging of cerebral lateralisation in animals. This is not necessarily an attack upon the dignity of man, though some people see it that way. Dignity is not something that a man has by virtue of his shape, or his size, or the stuff he is made of, or his mechanical complexity, or even his ancestry. It is rather something which depends on and reflects his capacity for interpersonal roles or relationships. It would be a false move to try and defend the dignity of man on the basis of some supposed uniqueness in his cerebral structure.

The increasing evidence of the links between the biochemical and anatomical structure of the brain and disordered mental life does not detract for one moment from the dignity of man. Rather it opens up the possibility for man to be treated in a more truly human way as, hopefully, new discoveries occur which enable us to deal with the biochemical changes which are producing the distressing mental symptoms.

— 4 —

Localising mind in brain

The approach of cognitive neuroscientists

There is more than one way of interpreting the evidence of the tightening link between mind and brain. Until relatively recently the gap between studies by neuroscientists investigating events occurring at the level of single cells and by psychologists studying processes like attention and thinking was so large that it seemed virtually unbridgeable—at least in the foreseeable future. There were, and still are, some neuroscientists who believe that the only way to make progress is to concentrate exclusively on the study of the most basic processes of neural functioning, what is sometimes called the 'bottom-up' approach. Other scientists are equally convinced that the only way to make real progress is to concentrate on gaining a deeper understanding of mental processes at the level of investigation of cognitive psychology; in their case a commitment to a 'top-down' approach.

In the past decade, however, another approach has led to a strengthening conviction within the scientific community that the time is now ripe for a fruitful convergence of research at these two different levels. This approach has become known as cognitive neuroscience. Those who take this view are convinced that there are clues from what is happening in research at one level

53

which can and must inform what is happening at other levels. What we discover at the one level helps us, they believe, to exclude false assumptions and sets limits to our model building at the other level. This kind of interaction, they say, is essential if we are to develop models that provide some understanding of what is actually happening in real brains rather than only simulating how particular kinds of machines could handle the same inputs and outputs as humans do. In cognitive neuroscientific research there is much talk about levels of analysis, levels of organisation and levels of processing. How do these differ and how do they relate to one another?

The importance of levels
There is a danger that the notion of levels may become so overworked that it becomes confusing rather than helpful. We shall, therefore, briefly examine three principal ways in which *levels* are referred to by cognitive neuroscientists. In so doing, we can explore to what extent they help and to what extent they confuse as we try to think about how to relate mental activities to brain processes.

Levels of analysis
When we look at an object we automatically and unthinkingly process a great deal of information about it. What is the nature of its surface? What is its shape and size? We also normally readily distinguish an object from its background? What part does shading play in this? What part do edges contribute? These seemingly simple questions turn out to be very complex and are of great interest to visual neuroscientists, psycho-physicists and cognitive psychologists. The specific question that each of these groups asks about a particular phenomenon, such as recognising an object against a background, will differ depending upon their own self-imposed research aims. It will also vary depending on the techniques of investigation they use and the kinds of models they are aiming to build of what is happening.

Perhaps the most influential approach of this kind was that spelled out by the late David Marr.[1] He made use of the notion of *levels* within computer science and in particular applied it to problems in the study of vision. In so doing, he suggested that there were at least three distinct levels of analysis and investigation which were important.

David Marr maintained that at the highest level there were computational problems which should be tackled in terms of an abstract analysis of what was going on. At this level questions would be asked about what are the main constituents of the task that is being performed. Secondly, he identified a level of analysis aimed at specifying, in a formal way, how you can ensure that there will be a correct output for a given input; what is called the level of the algorithm. And thirdly, he believed that analysis was required at the level of how the processes were actually implemented: what sort of physical material was doing the job and how did it work?

He noted that the algorithm, at the second level, is independent of the particular nature of the physical implementation involved. The physical components of the computer being used, for example, or of the nervous system are unimportant so long as the algorithm can run on them effectively. That, however, does not mean that if we are to discover how human beings *actually* carry out particular cognitive operations we can ignore knowledge of how the central nervous system is built and works. Indeed, a knowledge of how the brain is *actually* wired and works can be of crucial importance in devising plausible algorithms at the second level of analysis.

Levels of organisation
As one begins to consider the actual structure of the brain and the central nervous system we meet another way in which the notion of levels has been used by neuroscientists. The scale of the physical components of the nervous system targeted for investigation varies from the molecular up to pathways and systems extending over several metres. Figure 12, taken from a trend-setting paper by Churchland and Senjowski published in 1988[2], summarises and illustrates how the spatial extent of what is studied varies at the different levels. As can be seen, the variation covers several orders of magnitude. This alone should warn us that when, in a moment, we talk about the levels of implementation, we must remember that this diversity of structural levels will be matched by a diversity of algorithms which

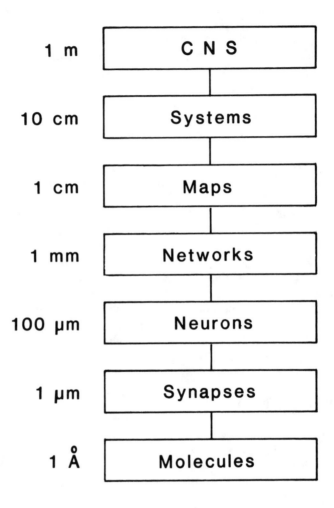

Figure 12 *Levels of organisation in the brain*

The scale of the physical components of the nervous system targetted for study by different investigators varies enormously from a metre down to the molecular level. Accounts given at one level do not make superfluous accounts given at other levels. Neural networks, in the middle of the hierarchy, may enable us to bring together results of investigations at the highest and lowest levels. (The figure is adapted from Churchland and Sejnowski 1986.)

aim to tell us how the tasks are being accomplished at that particular level. And, moreover, the study of a particular psychological phenomenon can be associated with accounts of what is happening at a variety of levels of implementation.

Levels of processing

There is yet one more common usage by neuroscientists of the notion of levels. It is levels of processing. Consider the information that is coming to you from the page in front of you. First there is a pattern of light and dark patches falling on the retinae of your eyes. Basic processing of this input goes on initially in your eyes at the retinal ganglion level. The information then travels on through your optic nerves to a nucleus in the brain known as the lateral geniculate nucleus. Here further processing occurs and the information thus processed passes, so to speak, further up stream to the cortex of your brain. From here it fans out to other parts of your cortex along so-called corico-cortical pathways and now much of the input is being processed in parallel. It is as if the mainstream has now split into many tributaries. But then just to complicate matters further we discover that, at these different processing levels, pathways go back downstream to centres at lower levels, so-called feedback projections. We do not yet understand the functions of these feedback pathways except that it is clear that what is happening at the higher levels can and does affect importantly what is coming upstream from the lower levels.

The need to recognise and do justice to what is happening at the higher levels of processing was one of the factors that so impressed the Nobel Laureate brain scientist Roger Sperry, that he could declare that a major revolution in our thinking about mind and brain has taken place in the past two decades. He commented, 'We do not look for conscious awareness in the nerve cells of the brain, nor the molecules or the atoms in brain processing.' He detected amongst neuroscientists 'a move away from the mechanistic, deterministic and reductionistic doctrines of the pre-1965 science to the more humanistic interpretations of the 1970s'.[3] As we shall see later, whilst Professor Sperry's own formulation of the mind/brain relationship is not without its problems, the fact remains that having worked at the leading

edge of the discipline with such great distinction, he firmly
believes that it is simplistic to try to reduce man to 'nothing but'
a physical-chemical machine. A view echoed in the lecture by
Lipowski referred to earlier when he criticised the oversimplistic
notion of what he called 'the reductionistic gospel'.

Neural networks and connectionist models

At the highest levels of mental functioning where choices are
made, some cognitive neuroscientists think of what is happening
in the brain in terms of interacting networks representing whole
systems of processing at work. They believe that it makes sense
to think about the brain as a mass of simple processing units
and interconnections. Mental processes are then thought to arise
through the myriad interactions of such units. Today 'neural
networks' have become one of the most actively researched areas
of cognitive science. So-called connectionist network models are
essentially *simplifying* models. Whilst trying to take account of
what is actually known about the structure and function of the
nervous system, they believe that the main constraints on their
model building are computational.

Connectionist models, or neural networks arose as cognitive
psychologists drew ideas and inspiration from computational
science. Connectionist models encompass many different forms.
Their primitive building blocks are simple processing units modelled abstractly on the neurone. These are arranged in layered
networks which are densely interconnected. Although single and
double layer systems are relatively simple to analyse and are
fairly powerful, the concentration today is on developing potentially more powerful (and complex) multilayered networks.
Figure 13 represents a three layer network featuring hidden units.
The processing units influence each other's values through connections that carry a numerical weight or strength. There are
three basic types of units. *Input units* encode input from sources
outside that part of the system. These may be, for example,
sensory input from the environment or information from other
parts of the processing system in which the network is contained.
The activations of the input units propagate along the connections until they impinge on the *output* units. The activation of
the output units encode the output that the system has computed

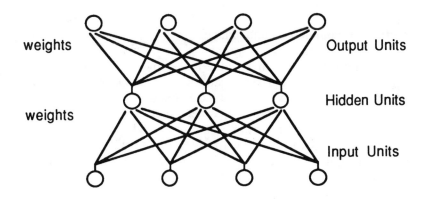

weights — Output Units

weights — Hidden Units

Input Units

Figure 13 *Schematic model of a simple three layered network*
More complex networks allow connections from a higher to a lower layer, and between units in the same layer. (Taken from Churchland and Sejnowski, 1989.)

Connectionist networks in a sense program themselves in that they contain procedures for adjusting the pattern of connectivity across the structure. When a network has one or more layers of hidden units (see above), the most widely used learning technique is so-called *back propagation of error*. This entails presenting the network with input activations and their corresponding correct target output activations. The system calculates an error signal on the basis of the discrepancy between the actual output of the system and the correct output. Connection strengths shown in the *weights* (above) are then modified in proportion to the product of the error and the input signal, which diminishes the probability of the same error being repeated.

from the input. In between the input and output units there may
be internal representation units or *hidden units* that participate
in representing neither the input nor the output of the network.
When the network is functioning many cells can be active
simultaneously. To describe the system at any one moment, the
set of simultaneous element activities is represented by a state
vector which corresponds to the cell's activation values. Different models make different assumptions about the level of activation that a unit can possess (for example, discrete or
continuous, bounded or unbounded).

Further technical details would be out of place here. Those
given so far are offered to give the reader the flavour of models
which are widely talked about and at times associated with an
unjustified aura or mystique. Some believe that the very term
neural networks is regrettable, others that it is a misleading
misnomer, since the properties of the units and the interconnections may have a very tenuous or no similarity with the properties of actual neurones and their interconnections. Neural
networks may show us what is possible but not necessarily what
is the case.

By comparison there are other models, sometimes called *realistic* models, which do make predictions about specific aspects
of nervous system dynamics. These models of actual neural
networks are motivated by biological constraints and by what
we actually know about the physiology and anatomy of nerve
cells. The hope is that the connectionist and realistic models will
gradually converge to give a more coherent account of the
mind/brain link. Not all cognitive psychologists agree that current neurological knowledge should constrain psychological theorising. However, the fact remains that much work in cognitive
science today does try to take account of what is currently
known about the structure and function of the nervous system.
Even so there are stringent criticisms already voiced that much
connectionist modelling and neural network research does not
in fact take sufficient account of such neurological knowledge.

Smolensky in 1988 reviewed connectionist work to see to
what extent it did take account of neurology.[4] He found clear
evidence that some neural networks did possess known characteristics of the cerebral cortex. But he also found features of

artificial neural networks which were not true of real brains. The Nobel Laureate Francis Crick and his colleagues have recently reviewed the relevance of neurology to connectionism.[5] They also find that in some respects they do not match up with what is actually known about, for example, how synapses work. Rather, some neural nets, they believe, violate known neurophysiological facts about synaptic processes.

We do not expect to construct a model that will cover all the levels of neural organisation discussed above. The fact that what is happening at one level may be explained in terms of what is happening at a lower level does not mean that the higher level model or theory is now useless or that the higher level phenomenon no longer exists. Explaining what is happening at one level is not the same as explaining away the phenomenon under investigation at that level. A fair assessment of these new advances in model building by cognitive neuroscientists would be that they are potentially exciting and rewarding but that in some quarters enthusiasm has outrun achievement. Time will tell their true worth. Whatever way it turns out their status will be yet another way of modelling the embodiment of mental events in physical substrates.

Localisation in cognitive neuroscience
Studies of the possible localisation of mental events in the brain look set to take significant steps forward as psychologists use new techniques which monitor the selective activity of different parts of the brain when cognitive tasks are being done. Underlying these approaches is the hypothesis that performing a cognitive task depends upon the integrated functioning of numbers of elementary operations and it is these latter that are strictly localised. Since many such local operations are involved in any cognitive task the activity in a corresponding set of distributed brain areas must be orchestrated into a coherent whole. The task is not performed by any single area in the brain, but the operations that underlie the performance are strictly localised. This way of thinking about localisation fits well with some of the connectionist and network models mentioned earlier.

A good example of the success of this kind of approach is Michael Posner's studies of reading and listening. Using the brain imaging technique known as Positron Emission Tomography (PET scan), they observed brain processes that were active during reading a single word. They discovered that different areas of the brain were activated depending on whether their subjects were *either* passively looking at nouns presented visually *or* actively generating a word and saying it aloud according to specific instructions such as an instruction to say aloud the use of an object named visually. So, presented with the word *hammer* they would say *hit* or *pound* or some such word. Another task they used was to say whether two words presented simultaneously rhymed. So, their subjects would see the words *pint-lint* or *row-though* and say whether they rhymed or not. Figure 14 illustrates this same phenomenon and is taken from a more recent study by Marcus Raichle.[6] As the caption indicates, it shows which different parts of the brain were selectively active depending on the nature of the cognitive task being done. So, once again, we have evidence of the mind/brain link but now suggesting a distributed rather than narrowly circumscribed form of localisation. The basic issue, however, remains the same, how do we think about this intimate relationship between the mind and brain so as to do justice to both aspects of the unified event? Reductionism is too simplistic because, whilst under the passively receiving tasks it may satisfy, it will not do in the other situations where what the subject is choosing to do is being revealed in the selective brain activity. Mind and brain both matter.

Two illustrative examples—attention and memory

Attending—a localised and distributed brain process
As Michael Posner and Steven Petersen have pointed out (1990), an understanding of how we attend to some things and not others—a very cognitive high level activity—has fascinated psychologists since the start of experimental psychology.[7] Today with developments in neuroscience of the kinds outlined above, such high level mental processes have been subjected to physiological analysis and even to identifying anatomical areas that seem to be basic to focal conscious processing.

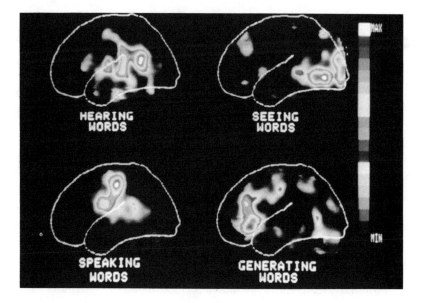

Figure 14 *How Positron Emission Tomography (PET) images help in studying the specialised functions of particular brain regions*

A series of PET scans indicates *changes* in local brain blood flow in the
normal human brain during the processing of words. By averaging PET images
it is possible to isolate cortical regions concerned with processing of words.
The four lateral views of the human brain shown here are averages of the
brain activities of nine normal subjects. The input components of language—
visually scanning a word or hearing it—activate the regions of the brain in
the upper two images. The output components of language and the thoughts
stimulated by this activate the regions shown in the lower two images.
(PET scans courtesy of Marcus Raichle, Professor of Radiology and Neurology, Mallinckrodt Institute of Radiology at Washington University, U.S.A.,
March 1993)

Attention, they believe, has a unique role in that it connects the mental level of description of processes used in cognitive science with the anatomical level common in neuroscience. For them, attention is an excellent example of the central role that mental concepts play in understanding brain functions as proposed by Roger Sperry,[8] whom they quote with approval.

Control from below upward is retained but is claimed to not furnish the whole story. The full explanation requires that one take into account new, previously nonexistent, emergent properties, including the mental, that interact causally at their own higher level and also exert causal control from above downward.

It offers a way into exploring causal control of brain systems by mental states. They speak of understanding 'how voluntary control is exerted over more automatic brain processes'.

Whilst acknowledging that their views are speculative and controversial, Posner and Petersen believe there is now a basis from which detailed studies of attention from a cognitive neuroscience viewpoint can take place. We shall not attempt to spell out their views in more detail here. It is very pertinent to our present discussion, however, to note how the fundamental findings to which they refer illustrate beautifully the convergent use by cognitive neuroscientists of concepts and models of the traditional localisationist kind described in earlier chapters and the recent 'networks' approaches discussed in this chapter.

Posner and Petersen identify what they call three 'fundamental findings'. First that 'the attention system of the brain is anatomically separate from the data processing systems that perform operations on specific inputs even when attention is oriented elsewhere. It interacts with other parts of the brain, but maintains its own identity.' Second that 'attention is carried out by a network of anatomical areas. It is neither the property of a single centre, nor a general function of the brain operation as a whole.' And third that 'the areas involved in attention carry out different functions, and these specific computations can be specified in cognitive terms.'

Bringing together studies of humans and of animals and the use of techniques of cerebral blood flow, Positron Emission

Tomography and lesion studies, they argue that a composite picture begins to emerge. In their paper they identify an anterior and a posterior attentional system in the brain.

The importance of Posner's and Petersen's ideas for our discussion is that they again emphasise and illustrate that there is nothing necessarily vague or unscientific in recognising the reality and importance of essentially cognitive operations of which attention is a prime example. Moreover, as Posner and Petersen have indicated, it gives one way into understanding how *voluntary* control is exerted over brain systems. The mind initiates activity which is reflected in discrete changes in different areas of the brain depending upon the task being undertaken.

Remembering

When we recognise that the higher levels of processing are networks of cells or, indeed, webs of interacting networks, we see that the notion of localisation of function, as discussed earlier, needs some revision. Distributed processing is now the key concept. But notice that because the way of thinking about the information processing function of the brain has changed, that, of itself, does not necessarily imply any diminution in the tightness of the mind/brain link.

The argument for an ever-tightening link between mind and brain, to which the evidence for localisation we reviewed earlier so clearly pointed, does not depend upon a particular kind of mind/brain embodiment for its force or validity. Theorising about the nature of the mind/brain link is moving fast at the present time. Workers following the approaches outlined in this chapter represent the link differently from that portrayed in our earlier chapters. For example, in his book, *Spatial Distributed Memory*, Panti Kanerva[9] points out that recent models by Marr, Albus, Rumelhart and Senjowski are characterised by their idea of memory as a stored pattern distributed over many cortical locations, with a single location partaking in the storage of many different patterns. They see retrieval of what is stored in memory as being by mathematical reconstruction from the contents of many such locations.

Kanerva writes,

In addition to the distributed models, localised models have been
proposed as models of human memory. Single memory location
or node of a localised model is associated with a single stored
pattern or concept. Of such models Baum, Moody & Wilczek's
(1986) sparse memory that creates a 'grandmother' cell for each
stored pattern is in some ways similar to my sparse distributed
memory, whereas the semantic-net models of Feldman & Ballard
(1982) are entirely different.

Kanerva's discussion of 'grandmother' cells brings to mind the
'grandmother' cells for which we saw evidence in the single cell
recording studies of face perception described in chapter two.

Kanerva believes that these distributed models are better able
to cope with hardware failures. They are good models in that
they reflect the remarkable resilience of brain functioning to
some kinds of extensive brain damage, despite which cognitive
capacities remain relatively intact. Kanerva comments,

> Common to all these models is that they can operate with
> imprecise and incomplete data and can construct from these data
> the most likely associated patterns. Therefore, they are all
> sensitive to similarity. Furthermore, the distributed models in
> particular are rather immune to hardware failures. According to
> these models, speed is obtained by making the circuits very large
> and doing many computations at once (that is, in parallel).

The relevance of Kanerva's model of memory to our discussions is that the tightening of the mind/brain link is not dependent upon a particular model since almost all current models
make the assumption that the mind is embodied in the workings
of the brain. The question is what is the nature of that embodiment?

The essential point is that each of these different ways of
thinking about the mind/brain link offer us ways of glimpsing
how what happens in the mind is embodied in what is happening
in the brain. What these new approaches do is caution us against
adopting oversimplistic views of localisation. They also underline how top down processes with feedback to lower levels are
crucial in determining what goes into the brain and how it is
processed. And here we come against real puzzles which will
take a long time to unravel. In so doing, we shall, as Churchland

and Senjowski concluded in their article, meet 'results that are likely to surprise us'.[10] Seldom has the open-mind been more essential in scientific enquiry than in this field.

—5—

Maintaining a balance

The effects of environment and experience

The importance of environment

So far our attention has been focused, almost exclusively, on the biological basis of our thinking and acting. By way of examples, we considered recent discoveries about possible biochemical bases of mental illnesses including schizophrenia. We also looked at some of the changes that take place in all of us as we grow old. These may, in some people, for as yet largely unknown reasons, lead to distressing changes in mental life such as dementia. Since we were interested in a better understanding of how the brain and the mind are linked, we looked in detail at the kinds of evidence that point to the localisation of mental functions in the brain. All in all, the evidence underlined what we had noted earlier, that almost every advance in psychology and neuroscience seems to tighten the link between mind and brain. But, of course, except for the very occasional hermit, none of us live our lives in social isolation, and even the hermit does not live his life in physical isolation. In this sense, we have been considering somewhat artificial situations and this we must now correct. To do so we shall examine how the environment, whether the physical or the social, interacts with us and affects our mental life and behaviour.

69

By way of illustration we shall consider the results of studies in three areas of research. In each case we shall be looking for answers to the same basic question of how someone's earliest environment may affect how she thinks, learns and behaves in later life.

Any attempt to study the effects of the environment on human beings is fraught with difficulties, not least because of the inevitable built-in differences between individuals due to genetic factors. This topic, therefore, is a good example of how psychological research depends on studies of animals. In the case of animals it is possible to ensure that, for example, they all have the same genetic background and that the physical environment is the same for them all, both before and after birth; something one certainly would not do with human beings.

The physical environment, brain and behaviour

The effects of the environment on behaviour as a topic of investigation, like so many of the topics we have discussed, is not new. In recent years, however, research has shown clearly that the nature of the environment in which an animal is reared has specific consequences for its later brain development and cognitive abilities. As work in this field developed, so different environmental factors were shown to produce both anatomical and biochemical changes in the brain, as well as having clear-cut behavioural consequences.

As long ago as 1949, the distinguished Canadian psychologist, Donald Hebb, had noticed that rats kept at his home as pets consistently out-performed laboratory rats on a whole series of learning tasks. Hebb's observations were extended systematically by other workers and their results supported the contention that early experience did affect the ability of animals to learn and to solve problems. The work done initially on rats has now been extended to a variety of other species. The general finding is that the enrichment of the environment improves learning later in life, but the effects of an impoverished environment have been less consistent.

In the classical experiments by Mark Rosenweig and his colleagues in California, they defined an enriched environment for a laboratory rat as living in large cages with groups of twelve to fifteen other animals. The rats had the opportunity for contact with a variety of objects which were put into their cage and with which they could supposedly 'play'. These animals thus received social stimulation from the other animals living in the cage and from playing with the toys with which they were housed. They were also stimulated by the things they saw and heard in the environment outside the cage. By contrast, their litter mates in the impoverished environment lived alone in cages that had solid walls on three sides. Thus they could not see other animals and they lived continually in quiet rooms with low illumination. Both groups received the same diet of food and water.

It was discovered that at maturity the brains of the animals brought up in the enriched environment differed from those reared in the impoverished environment. Such things as the weight of the cerebral cortex, and the length and width of the cerebral hemispheres were greater in the brains of the animals reared in the enriched environment. This appeared to be due to an increase in cell size, in the number of glial cells (the cells packed around the nerve cells in the brain) and to a much greater degree of branching of the dendrites of the cells in the cortical areas. Consistent with these anatomical changes, there were also reports of biochemical differences. For example, there were greater levels of RNA (ribonucleic acid) activity in the brains of the animals from the enriched environment. It was also found that some neurotransmitters, the brain's chemical messengers, varied in concentration. For example, acetylcholine, one of the principal neurotransmitters in some nerve tissue, was increased in the brains of the animals brought up under impoverished conditions. The concentration of acetylcholinesterase was less in the brains of the animals brought up in the enriched environment. Thus the results of rearing these animals in the enriched or impoverished environment was linked to alterations in the so-called cholinergic system in the brains.

These early studies have been extended by workers at the University of Illinois, who have reported that giving animals extended learning experiences seems to produce changes in the neural tissue in those parts of the brain where the learning experience is most likely to be processed. They interpret this as indicating that, in general, the activated neural connections are

consolidated and preserved whilst unused connections degener-
ate. More and more researchers are becoming convinced that the
neural connections in brains are indeed dynamic from birth
onwards, and before, and thus our neural tissue is constantly
changing. It seems that experience at the right time and of the
right kind helps to nurture what nature has provided.

Some illustrative examples

Nutritional deprivation

In the last few years our television screens and newspapers have
thrust upon us horrific photographs of desperate starvation in
some African countries. Anyone aware of the effects of malnutrition on brain growth immediately wonders how, and in what
way, the children affected by famine in the very early weeks of
life may have been penalised for life in their subsequent mental,
as well as physical, development.

The effects of deprivation can operate either before or after
birth. To deprive any organism of food for a sustained length of
time produces a sharp drop in body weight. If we do the same
thing with an adult, brain-weight remains relatively unimpaired.
The body, it would seem, is willing to sacrifice every other organ
in order to protect the brain. The adult story, however, is not
the same as the infant story. Studies of animals have shown that
newborns malnourished at times when normally there would be
rapid brain growth exhibit drastic drops in body weight and in
their brain's rate of growth. Evidence from such studies points
to the conclusion that, even if such an animal is subsequently
allowed to eat as much as it can, its brain growth may never
catch up.

Human researches on the effects of malnutrition are more
ambiguous in their conclusions. On the one hand, a study of
thousands of adults who as infants had survived months of
severe famine in a part of the Netherlands sealed off by the
Nazis at the end of World War II indicated that these infants did
not experience any lasting physical or intellectual damage so
long as they were well cared for after the war. They were just
as tall and intellectually capable as their contemporaries. On the
other hand, a study of African teenagers who had been chroni-

cally malnourished as infants showed that intellectually they were impaired compared with other teenagers from the same socioeconomic class and tribe who had been adequately nourished. Thus whilst severe short-term malnutrition does not cause irreparable damage, severe and long-lasting malnutrition can cause intellectual as well as physical deficits. There are encouraging signs which indicate that where social and nutritional deprivation has occurred early, but has been permanently alleviated, there seems to have been a reversal of the earlier difficulties in mental activity.

Early experiences
In a sense the effects of malnutrition on the development of the brain, whilst a very serious problem, are not surprising. By comparison, the results of studies on the effects of quite short periods of stimulation on organisms during infancy are anything but expected. It seems that even mild sources of stress such as handling for a few minutes, if these occur during critical periods of infancy, can profoundly affect later behaviour. Such effects seem often out of all proportion to the stimulating events themselves. To be more specific, when animals that have been handled during infancy are subsequently put into situations which would normally provoke fear and anxiety, they react much less strongly than other animals, showing less fear and a capacity for faster learning.

However, the story is still only half-complete and many problems remain. It seems, for example, going back to the studies of Rosenweig and his colleagues, that some of the changes occurring in the brain such as the biochemical effects can be reversed by intensive environmental stimulation even after there has been a prolonged period of deprivation in early life. To draw parallels with the human situation is a hazardous business. We could at least note, however, that where children come from impoverished environments, they are likely to suffer *both* nutritional *and* environmental deprivation and, therefore, the effects we have noted may be compounded.

Early environment and later social behaviour
What happens very early in life affects not only learning abilities

and the development of the brain, but also subsequent social behaviour. Again, we have early classical studies as well as later confirmatory ones. Professor Harry Harlow many years ago, studying monkeys, observed that when they were reared without their mothers or without adequate substitute mothers they failed to develop normal social relations when they grew up. It is important, however, not to jump too readily to conclusions from this sort of work and to say that the social behaviour of a person is determined entirely by experiences happening in the first few weeks or months of life. The evidence certainly does not support such a conclusion.

A few years ago, Professor A D B Clarke and his wife Ann, published a book entitled *Early Experience: Myth and Evidence*.[1] In it they showed what a conceptual minefield it is when you try to disentangle the seemingly conflicting evidence from studies of the effects of early environment on later development. They point out that there is today a 'received wisdom' which says that the first few years of life are of vital long-term importance, but they caution that this view is held so strongly in some quarters that people are able only to see this effect and thus miss contrary evidence. For example, there are many studies showing that children who experience their growing up years in the same home are hardly more alike, in personality, than any two randomly paired individuals.

There is other evidence from, for example, studies of pre-school intervention which almost without exception show a substantial increase in intelligence and other cognitive abilities *during* such programmes. If the programme finishes there may be a progressive deceleration in IQ so that after four years the children involved are back to the baseline they would have been at without such intervention. Where any increases in IQ are apparent, three or four years after intervention has ended it seems that this is due not to the programme as such but to some more enduring changes in the relations between the parents and the children.

Returning briefly now to the extension of the early studies of Professor Harlow on the effects of early experiences on later social and emotional competence, we can ask how do such early life experiences affect us? Studies of children who grow up in good, well-equipped and well-staffed institutions show that the supposed and demonstrated undesirable outcomes of institutionalisation need not be as great or as enduring as the earlier much publicised views of workers like Professor John Bowlby had implied. They still demonstrate, however, the adverse effects of some kinds of early experience. For example, the institutional children studied by Professor Tizard from 1974 to 1978 showed an ability to catch up with the normal children on tests of mental ability and language ability but they continued to show other enduring and more diffuse changes in behaviour in such things as the way in which they all the time sought to gain attention in school. As Dr Michael Rutter said recently, these children were usually 'more attention-seeking, more restless, more disobedient and unpopular'.

That the interpretation of the effects of separation has to be done with caution is underlined by a number of additional studies. The effect of separating a child from his parents, because of divorce or marital separation is different from separation of the child from a parent because of the parent's death. In one study, it was found that only divorce and marital separation showed any association with later delinquency whereas death of a parent was not related in this way. Similarly, Rutter examined the relationship between the quality of parental marriage and the incidence of anti-social behaviour in the children. He found a linear relationship between the two variables so that children showing anti-social behaviour were more likely to have parents with a very poor marriage. He also compared the incidence of delinquency in children who had been separated from their parents because of physical illness with those who had been separated because of family discord or psychiatric illness. The incidence of delinquent behaviour was some four times higher in the second group. All this underlines the fact that the effects of separation depend upon the meaning of the separation and the circumstances surrounding it.

Professor Clarke and his wife, in the book mentioned above, after reviewing the literature in this field concluded that, as yet, there is no clearly developed model of how physical and social environments affect children during the course of growth and much work remains to be done. On balance, however, they believe that it seems that one should think in terms of the effect of certain critical events. Apart from events which may make it absolutely impossible to sustain life, it would appear that there is no psychosocial adversity to which some children have not been subjected and yet have later recovered, *provided there has been a radical change in circumstances.* They believe that the evidence points to the need for a greater recognition of the possibility of personal change following misfortune.' This is an important conclusion because it helps to counterbalance the otherwise pessimistic conclusion to which earlier work has consistently pointed. The importance of personal attitudes and personal beliefs is something we shall take up a little later on.

Some recent developments

The recent and ongoing work of Robert Hinde and his wife Joan Stevenson-Hinde at Cambridge provides an excellent example of how the results of careful studies of animals and humans converge and lead to a better understanding of the effects of the social and interpersonal environment on behaviour and the functioning of the brain.

Working on both rhesus monkeys and humans, Robert Hinde conducted a series of studies concerned to assess aspects of the effects of early relationships. Some years ago Kosterlitz had demonstrated the importance of naturally occurring opiates in the human body, the so-called endogenous opiates, and Robert Hinde and his coworkers investigated the possible importance of these substances for the development of mother/infant relationships. Their working hypothesis was that one of those endogenous opiates, the brain's beta-endorphin-containing system provided a reward for social behaviour. They proposed that either under-activation or over-activation of this system due to social and environmental circumstances, may have effects on the infant's bond with its mother and may also have long-term consequences for the development of the infant's relationship with its peers. They showed that social interactions of monkeys had significant consequences for beta-endorphin in the cerebrospinal fluids (CSF) of the animals studied and that the levels in the CSF could be related to the behaviour of individual animals. They showed that although a multiplicity of functions can be attributed to the brain's beta-endorphin system, nevertheless they all have in common behavioural reward and the psychological, endocrine and automatic consequences of reward or non-reward. They showed that social interaction not only acquires the status of rewarding behaviour, but in so doing it carries with it the risk of disruption of this system in the event of social breakdown, and with that a series of malfunctions may occur to primary motivated behaviour, things such as sexual behaviour, feeding and maternal behaviour.

With children, the influence of close relationships on individual development has been the subject of intensive study for many years as was indicated above. Stevenson-Hinde's own studies had already demonstrated links between 'shyness' and the interactions going on within a family. The essential point of these kinds of studies is that they point to an intimate relationship between the behaviour of the organism, in this case the mother/infant link, and the infant's link with other infants, and the naturally-occurring chemicals in the brain. Where, for example, there has been stress resulting from the infant being separated from the mother, it has been shown in guinea pigs and puppies, that the administration of opiates can alleviate this stress. Conversely, other studies, this time using rodents and dogs, have reported that where opiate receptors in the brain are blocked, this interferes with normal maternal behaviour and disrupts pup retrieval behaviour, characteristic of rodents and dogs. In addition, it has been shown in monkeys that the beta-endorphin system is actually activated by social grooming.

For the purposes of our present discussion, the take-home message from the studies of Robert Hinde and Joan Stevenson-Hinde, and others like them, is that something so seemingly unphysiological as social interaction between mother and infant, and between one infant and another, can produce changes in the biochemical substrates of brain function which have both short-term and possibly long-lasting consequences. Moreover, these longer-lasting consequences can, it seems, in some situations, be reversed by the administration of the depleted beta-endorphins. The animal studies, for example, make it clear that when an infant is separated from its mother and emits the typical distress calls which go with such separation, these can be reduced by administering opiate agonists or made more intense by administering opiate antagonists.

Brain, mind and lifestyle
A recent report entitled *The Health and Life-Style Survey*, provides a good example of the power of 'top-down' factors, of how what we think about ourselves and others affects our health and, thus, bodily processes.

It goes without saying that an individual's well-being is related not only to physical health but to mental health and mental functioning. We saw in earlier chapters that with identifiable changes in brain structure there come distressing changes in mental health and mental functioning. But in addition to the influence which health, behaviour and circumstances can exert on how we think and feel (so-called cognitive functioning), we have to remember that cognitive functioning itself exerts an influence on health. A high level of cognitive functioning may, for example, be associated with the avoidance of accidents, with health-seeking behaviour, and with an increased ability to benefit from health education. Conversely, where cognitive functioning is impaired this may be associated with increased risks to health and a reduced ability to benefit from advice available about health practices.

The example of coronary heart disease—first ideas and second thoughts
A topic of much public interest in recent years in this general area of the relationship between physical health and an individual's mental health and personality has been the suggested relationship between some forms of behaviour which were said to be better predictors of coronary heart disease than others. In both cross-sectional and longitudinal studies it has been found that people who, on various questionnaire measures, were shown to be unusually ambitious, always in a hurry and generally working under a time-imposed stress (so-called Type A behaviour) were also those who showed an increased likelihood of suffering from coronary heart disease. There is also evidence that the mental state and personality of the individual may be related to the prognosis. All this makes good sense because it

fits with the common view that physical illness and disability can be overcome more effectively by people who are in the right frame of mind. Further work on the Type A personality indicated that it is not the ambition and time-consciousness that's toxic but the proneness to irritability and anger in such people.

There are, of course, many ways in which personality and health may interact. Personality characteristics may predispose some people to certain forms of lifestyle or certain types of diseases; conversely, circumstances in which people find themselves, their lifestyle or poor health may influence their personality. *The Health and Lifestyle Survey* just referred to reported research carried out in Cambridge, England by an interdisciplinary team. The results of the research and the analysis carried out so far, whilst in part supporting the earlier work on so-called Type A behaviour which is related to heart disease, nevertheless showed that when age and socioeconomic group were properly taken into account there was no evidence of a relationship between scores of Type A questionnaires and heart disease. The authors of the report, however, cautioned that this finding should be interpreted carefully since one of the chief reasons for it may be that individuals with serious heart disease were unlikely to have been included in their particular survey.

What was clearly confirmed in this study was the importance of social contact and support for individual health; a finding long recognised by anthropologists and sociologists. Two longitudinal studies had included indicators of the extent of social contacts in the individuals involved. One of these reported that people who lacked social and community ties were more likely to die in the nine-year follow-up period than those with more extensive contacts. Moreover, the association between social ties and mortality was found to be independent of self-reported physical health status at the time of the original survey, socioeconomic status and health practices such as smoking, alcohol consumption, obesity, physical activity and utilisation of preventative health services, as well as a cumulative index of health practices. A quite separate study reported that after appropriate adjustments for age and a variety of risk factors for mortality, men who reported a high level of social relationships and activities were significantly less likely to die during the follow-up period. These results were found to apply regardless of age, occupation and health status. The Cambridge report concludes that,

> It is clearly demonstrated that—however the concept is defined and measured—social support or integration is a factor in both physical and mental pursuit of health. The effect on psychosocial health, or malaise, is stronger than that upon physical fitness, but physical symptoms are certainly more frequent among those who feel themselves socially isolated and unsupported.

Learned helplessness
One much publicised set of researches in this area is subsumed under the label of 'learned helplessness'. The leading researcher in this field is Martin Seligman. He defines learned helplessness as, 'When a person is faced with an outcome that is independent of his responses, he learns that the outcome is independent of his responses.' In a study typical of those carried out by Seligman and subsequently by others, animals have been put into situations in which they discover that their behaviour cannot provide an escape from slight electric shocks. Such animals later failed to take an initiative in other situations when in fact they could escape and avoid punishment. In contrast, animals which are taught personal control by successfully escaping any first shocks are found to adapt easily to a new situation. Seligman has pointed to similarities in human situations such as when depressed or oppressed people become passive about their situation because they believe that whatever they do, their actions can make no difference.[3]

One frequently quoted study, which is a good example of human research in this area, was done by Rodin and Langer and serves to illustrate this group of researches.[4] They began by suggesting that one of the reasons why many elderly people living in institutions were debilitated was because they saw themselves as having no control of their situation. Rodin and Langer studied the residents of a nursing home and began by randomly assigning them to one of two matched groups. One group was briefed by the staff in a way which stressed the staff's responsibilities for them and their activities. The other group was given instructions that emphasised the residents' sense of their own control of what they did and of their own destiny. The results of the study were striking. Those in the group in which personal control had been stressed reported significant increases in their personal happiness only three weeks later. Independently, the nurses' and physicians' judgments matched the subjects' own reports. Eighteen months later the effect was still evident. Most striking of all, whereas 30% of the low responsibility group had died, the corresponding figure for the high responsibility group was only 15%.

Some people have generalised these findings and speculated that the psychological teaching given in colleges for the last two decades, which it is claimed has tended to emphasise the very strong effects of environmental control to the exclusion of other factors, may have led to an increased sense of powerlessness amongst many people in their formative years. It was argued that if the young college students believed that the forces that constrain their development were all important, then understandably they could feel powerless to do anything about such forces.

Thus, a whole range of findings in this area of research on subjects from helpless dogs to residents of institutions all confirm the extreme consequences of losing one's sense of personal control over the environment. The explanation of the results of these experiments is far from settled, but it will continue to be an important area of research. Those who work in the field believe that in looking at ourselves and understanding ourselves, we should realise the importance of our beliefs about our personal freedom, and remember that we tend to become what we imagine ourselves to be—a further underlining of the importance of 'top down' factors. Freedom is not just a matter of resisting or relieving pressures upon us of an environmental kind but also of our own internal beliefs. As Professor David Myers has put it: 'People who believe they have response-ability act with more responsibility.'[5]

Taking stock: hidden assumptions and exaggerated claims
We have seen some of the demonstrated effects of the physical and social environment which, together with our genetic endowment, shape our behaviour and set limits to our capacities. We have also noted the accumulating evidence pointing to the crucial

importance for our personal well-being and behaviour, of how we see ourselves and our relation to our environment. These two emphases are complementary and not conflicting. Each is true and each is valid. We are both the creatures and the creators of our environments. Both must be taken into account if we are to do justice to the total evidence. But what implications do they have for a proper assessment of ourselves and our freedom?

It is clear that all of us, all the time, make implicit assumptions about our own freedom and about other people's freedom. Such assumptions have consequences and lead to actions. To be sure, psychologists do not do very well at predicting and controlling people's behaviour. The unaccounted-for variations in our data, the so-called error factor in our results, remain uncomfortably large. In practical terms, too, our attempts at, for example, rehabilitation of persistent offenders leaves a great deal to be desired; presumably we should do much better if our knowledge was as firmly based as some suppose. Were we as successful in controlling and manipulating the determinants of behaviour as some would have you believe we should be much better placed to offer solutions to some of our more pressing social problems. Without doubt the importance of a detailed understanding of the environmental forces at work is important for a proper understanding of the effects on us and our children, of our schools, our homes, our churches and other familiar social institutions.

What may be an appropriate strategy for a psychologist to adopt in his research may be an entirely inappropriate one for him to adopt as his own dominant self-image and the one that he should commend to others.

As we have considered the findings, from the diversity of approaches available today in the study of human nature, we have become aware of how, by concentrating solely on certain 'bottom-up' scientific approaches, we may lose sight of man as a whole. Lipowski reminded us that history teaches: 'That human behaviour cannot be explained or predicted from any single theoretical standpoint' and 'We need to bring together facts and hypotheses from three mutually irreducible vantage points—the psychological, the biological and the sociological'.[6] We must put the individual together again at some point if we are not to finish up by deceiving ourselves. Sadly, the tone of some reports of scientific approaches to the study of man are intemperate. If one has a high view of human nature, whether it be held within a humanistic or a religious framework, some of these intemperate, and I would say unscientific, extrapolations may appear to threaten the dignity of man.

Beware—people studying people

Are there limits to the scientific study of persons?
We quite rightly look back with breathtaking admiration to the Greeks and all their magnificent intellectual and cultural achievements. We owe them so much. The question remains, however, why was it that with such remarkable contributions to knowledge they still failed to initiate and sustain the rise of science 2,000 years ago? Why did the scientific revolution not begin in earnest until the 16th century and what allowed it to flourish from then onwards?

Any brief account, such as we have time for now, risks all the dangers of caricature and oversimplification. We must, even so, attempt it, if only to set what follows in a proper context and historical perspective. Historians of science point out how in the centuries immediately preceding the 16th, an attitude towards the natural world began to emerge which was to set the stage for the emergence of modern science. At that time two major influences, we are told, can be detected. The influences of Greek thinking and the influence of Hebrew/Christian thinking. These two streams of thought which had flowed together many centuries before had interacted from time to time, each altering the other slightly.

The emergence of the scientific method

The salient features of the view of nature which became a
catalyst for the development of science are well summarised by
contrasting them with those which characterised the Greek view.
Whilst for the Greek creation was divine and eternal, for this
other view, the Hebrew/Christian, the world is not eternal. It is
created and dependent upon God for its continuing moment by
moment existence. Nature and the divine are not to be identified
with one another but rather to be sharply separated. Secondly,
and as an outworking of this characteristic, because the natural
order is not divine it is not autonomous. Whereas for the Greek
the workings of nature were rationalistic and purposive with the
purposefulness firmly embedded within nature itself, by contrast
in the Hebrew/Christian tradition purpose resides not in nature
but in God who creates and sustains the natural order. Thus the
important implication follows that if a man wishes to discover
the patterns of order in nature he must have recourse to experience, to observation and experiment, because he cannot discover
them by intuition or reason alone. A further contrast we may
make is that *man, mind and all, is part of the created order.*
The mind of man is not divine. It is subject to error and thus it
cannot infallibly intuit or read off from nature the inherent
qualities of nature.

The majority of historians of science are now agreed that these
features were crucial to the beginning and the sustained development of science. And they were to have important consequences for the development of a further understanding of man
and his nature. What was true of the developments, beginning
with Galileo, concerning the natural order generally, later
became true of the specialist interest in the nature of man. A
proper use, as Galileo showed, of the rationalistic approach in
conjunction with experimentation, could lead to significant scientific advances. The experimental approach found its true
champion, however, in men like Francis Bacon. To Baconians
nature was not logical and rational but given. And according to
Bacon, we forfeit our dominion over nature by wanting to make
her conform to our rationalist prejudices instead of adapting our
conceptions to the data of observations and experiment. Bacon
thus learned and demonstrated the lesson that we should 'seek

for the sciences not arrogantly in the little cells of human wit, but with reverence in the greater world'.

By the 19th century yet another accepted tenet of Aristotelian doctrine was to come under scrutiny and under fire. It had seemed 'natural' and 'reasonable' to conclude from Aristotle's teaching that since all living things are in some sense embodiments of external forms of unchanging essences, species are therefore fixed and unchanging. Now, however, with Darwin's teaching, Aristotelian biology was to be shaken to its very foundations. What if species are not fixed? What if there is a measure of change from generation to generation? Thus we find that what Newton had done to Aristotelian physics, Darwin was about to do to Aristotelian biology. With this challenge Darwin, like Newton, was to produce work which became the point of departure for a new world view. Newton's intelligently designed machine would, under Darwin's influence, acquire the properties of a dynamic and progressive process.

It may seem strange to us today to see how aspects of Darwin's view were in fact recapturing a true Hebrew/Christian emphasis of the nature of man. Nature, said Darwin, includes both man and his culture. By contrast, the Greek tendency had been to separate man from the rest of creation and to give him and his mind an arrogant, aristocratic place over against nature.

In earlier chapters we have, on several occasions, noted in passing, how scientists, equally competent, equally knowledgeable, have interpreted the same scientific evidence in different ways. This applies in the field of brain science as much as, if not more than, other areas of contemporary science. Since knowledge derived by brain scientists is at the same time knowledge about themselves, we should, perhaps, not be surprised to discover that when the wider implications of scientific findings come under discussion, the interpretations we meet are as much influenced by deeply held, personal non-scientific beliefs, as by the scientific findings as such. For this reason, we turn briefly now to look at how values interact with the practice and with the interpretation of the findings of science.

The pervasive influence of values in the scientific enterprise
Many, if not most, scientists as they go to their laboratories each

day, enjoy the work they do, hoping and possibly believing that some of its fruits will benefit society and the world in which they live. And at times they get considerable satisfaction from what they have achieved at the end of the day. This same majority of working scientists may be totally unaware of the hundreds of papers written by philosophers of science on 'the scientific method' or of the continuing debate about whether or not science is or can be a value-free enterprise. They have never doubted that it was some of their personal values which led them into science in the first place; that some of their current personal values influence their selection from the enormous range of problems that they could work on if they so choose; that their values also influence the decisions they make about when and where to publish their results; and that their values may also influence the suggestions that they put forward about the possible implications and applications of the results of their scientific research. This has all seemed so obvious that it has hardly been worth saying. And yet they now discover some people getting terribly excited because they have suddenly discovered that the scientific enterprise is not a totally value-free enterprise.

Is there value-free knowledge?
In an earlier chapter the scientific enterprise was portrayed as a map-making process that reflects our values. This does not mean, however, that the map itself reflects our values. To suggest that the map itself is affected by our values is a confusion perpetu- ated today in some quarters and we must deal with it in more detail now.

Values and the mapmaker
The maps that we find most useful are those that are reliable guides to the territory in which we live or which we wish to explore. The one who made the maps I now use could know nothing about my personal values nor those of the myriads of other people who may wish to use his maps. His values and beliefs may be quite different from my own but if his map is accurate I can still use it. There is nothing arbitrary therefore about wanting a map which is free from values. In this sense, the scientist's commitments to scientific detachment, in so far

as his accounts and theories may be regarded as maps, should be perfectly understandable. If he is doing his job properly his map should be useable by anyone regardless of what their personal values are.

As a scientist maps out the territory he investigates it is made up of both events and entities and it is a world where one thing causes another. He sees his map as the product of something more than mere stamp-collecting; more than the aggregation of a whole lot of disconnected observations. Rather, he wants to see some correlations between the events he observes and the interacting causes which he can identify. And therefore, unlike the geographical map or even the road map that helps us to get from say Sydney to Melbourne, our maps will not only describe the land of scientific endeavour but also offer explanations of what is found along the way and predictions about what may be found next. The laws that we describe will be prescriptive in the sense that they tell us what we ought to expect in a given set of circumstances on the basis of observations made in the past. They cannot, of course, ahead of time, assure us that unprecedented events may not occur but if they do we are obliged to justify any expectations that we had to the contrary. So far, so good. There has been little place for values so far in what I have said and the emphasis has all been on the map as being a value-free account. In this sense it epitomises the value-free objective knowledge talked about by some philosophers of science.

However, science is not just an abstraction as several commentators have underlined. For example, Ian Barbour has written, 'There are no bare, uninterpreted data . . . Man supplies the categories of interpretation, right from the start.' Michael Polanyi comments in similar vein, 'Viewed from the outside as we described him the scientist may appear as a mere truth-finding machine steered by intuitive sensitivity. But this takes no account of the curious fact that he is himself the ultimate judge of what he accepts as true. . .The scientist appears acting here as detective, policeman, judge and jury all rolled into one.' Or, from a non-scientist's and a different perspective, we have the comment by C S Lewis that 'What we learn from experience depends on the kind of philosophy we bring to experience.' This is well illustrated from the history of psychology. What was acceptable data to the psychoanalyst Sigmund Freud is quite different from what was acceptable data to the behaviourist B F Skinner. In this sense certainly it is true that our observations are all theory laden. Science is then an activity of people labelled scientists. They are people like you and me. They also have values which guide their thinking and behaving moment by moment. Just how these values are at work in the scientific enterprise is worthy of further consideration. Those sciences which aim at understanding human nature are perhaps especially vulnerable to the risk of having personal values smuggled in to the interpretation of the scientific data.

Values in the practice of science

The basic aim or goal of science is to understand the world around us. This understanding is then encapsulated or summarised in our theoretical knowledge. Empirical facts can often support *several* incompatible theoretical positions and in any case, observations in science are dependent upon theory. One could never choose between competing theories by simply looking at the brute facts or allowing the facts to speak for themselves, as an extreme positivist position in the past would have held. All scientists have values which are reflected in the criteria they employ for making choices between competing theoretical explanations. The hope is that by systematically employing these values their theoretical explanations will move closer and closer to the ideal of what has been called the 'horizon-concept' of truth. In support of this view, reference is made to the history of science which is there for all to see.

As Van Till[1] has pointed out, the values scientists apply when choosing between theories include the following. First, the predictive accuracy of the theory. Whilst in the short run some lack of fit between the predictions and the realities may be permitted, in the long run the theory ought to demonstrate predictive accuracy if it is to be accepted. Second, the theory must show some sort of internal coherence, that is to say, it ought to hang together without any, or with very few, loose ends. Thirdly, it must meet a criterion of external consistency. In other words, it must be consistent with other related theories and fit in the general background of scientific theorising. It shouldn't contradict theories from other related disciplines which are clearly akin to it. Fourthly, the theory ought to have some sort of unifying power by bringing together areas of knowledge which previously were seemingly disconnected. Fifthly, it ought to prove to be fertile ground for new and imaginative developments. Finally, it should have some sort of simplicity. Simplicity in this sense is that it should have some sort of aesthetic appeal which may be felt and appreciated by experts within the field. The oft-quoted example here is Einstein and his theory of relativity. Different scientists attach different values to these criteria, the question is asked, if this is so in what sense does science remain objective? It is these values, after all, which underlie our conviction that scientific knowledge, for the moment, represents a secure basis of knowledge within which we can hope to understand the world in which we live.

Motives in the practice of science

It is not surprising that the motives that different scientists have for starting a piece of work, continuing it, and bringing it to successful completion, will to some extent, reflect the values which they hold most strongly and deeply. This should cause us no surprise. It does not, however, mean that the end product of what is achieved will necessarily be value-laden simply because the motives that kept one going were value-laden. There is no necessary logical connection between these at all. At the same time, it is obviously nonsense to suggest that the practice of science is value-neutral. Every decision we make about whether to publish, when to publish and at what time we should lift the lid on a particular discovery is fully value-laden, as all human judgments must be. However, for the working scientist in chemistry or physics or physiology or in many areas of psychology, to then suggest that because his practice of science cannot be value-free, therefore the ideal that he holds of there being value-free knowledge should now be dismissed as a myth, is a complete nonsequitur.

Motives and values also come into play in deciding how best to present the products of our scientific endeavour. When to judge that they are at a stage when they are worth communicating to others and where that communication should take place will all involve personal values. This will be especially so if there is a degree of uncertainty still about one's final conclusions from the scientific data and even more so if the data are readily susceptible to misreporting and misrepresentation.

It is difficult to understand where this demand for us to decry the possibility and the ideal of value-free knowledge comes from. Some have suggested that it comes more from those who study human nature and human society than those who study the inanimate physical world.

When values come disguised as facts

Social scientists, it is said, are especially vulnerable to the temptation to expound values in the guise of facts. There are, sad to say, numerous instances of this. For example, it is not long since a great stir occurred when the American psychiatrist, Thomas Szasz, pointed out that mental illness is all too easily defined not in medical terms as are other illnesses, but in terms of deviant communicational behaviour. The film, *One Flew Over the Cuckoo's Nest*, became a graphic illustration of this. Or, to take another example, twenty years ago we seldom heard of school children suffering from 'learning disabilities'. Today, however, we are told that in North America there are literally millions of 'learning disabled children' in schools. Whilst we must be careful not to too readily dispute this fact because there are doubtless some who are handicapped by brain disorders, nevertheless we may still wonder if such a diagnostic label is not sometimes misapplied. It is too readily applied to the children rather than to the school. Perhaps 'learning disabilities' should always be put alongside 'teaching disabilities'.

Or, again, consider how readily people are referred to today as mature or immature. So often such labels are really nothing but disguised value judgments. To take a related recent example, it is not sufficiently well recognised that the characteristics of so-called 'self-actualised' people as described by Abraham Maslow are little more than a statement of Maslow's own personal values. The initial selection of a self-actualised person to be studied was done on a subjective basis by Maslow himself.

Such descriptions are not inherent in nature, they are the creation of Maslow's mind.

The about-face that took place in the US Government's official pamphlet on infant care between 1938 and 1942 is another instance of personal beliefs posing as facts. The same change in views can be detected by looking at the early and late writings of Benjamin Spock. Spock's commonsense book of baby and childcare became the world's third leading bestseller for a while. However, after research showed that student activists of the late 1960s tended to come from relatively permissive and democratic homes, even Benjamin Spock was led to reflect upon the wisdom of his earlier advice. In his latest edition, Benjamin Spock now explicitly informs the reader at the start of his personal goals for children.

We see then that there are special problems for psychologists. Writing as a medical practitioner, Elliot Freidson, has argued, 'The profession's role in a free society should be limited to contributing the technical information men need to make their own decisions on the basis of their own values. When he pre-empts the authority to direct, even constrain men's decisions on the basis of his own values, the professional is no longer an expert but rather a member of a new privileged class disguised as an expert.'

Are there special problems for human and social science?
Those working in the so-called human sciences face particular problems not met by those working with the inanimate world. In the first place, they themselves are people investigating people and as such their own interests, values and ideologies, their own ideas of what it is or ought to be like to be a person living in a particular society, easily colour, not only what seems to be worth investigating, but also how they perceive it. It is understandable, for example, that those who use questionnaires recognise that it is seldom a neutral activity. The very idea of asking questions of other people is a hazardous one, since the questions asked (as any effective advocate knows) so easily shape the answers that one may receive. In that sense questioning in a value-free way becomes virtually impossible.

Once you begin to make your findings known amongst those

whom you have been investigating it will, in general, make it more difficult for them to act in an unselfconscious way. This is a bit like the notorious self-fulfilling effects of opinion polls taken during elections. As the information is fed back to those whose opinions have been sampled so their subsequent views may be affected by the information that is fed back to them. Once you predict to a group of people how they are likely to vote in any election you are not so much just telling them about themselves but you may well be manipulating their subsequent behaviour. Though this effect has not been strongly confirmed, it does remain the case that polls do affect political fortunes by, for example, directing contributions and enthusiasms and media coverage towards those who look like winners.

Without a doubt then, the social scientist faces particular problems not faced by the biologist or physical scientist. For example, if you are a social scientist with a specialist research interest in counselling you will find it difficult to exclude your personal values from the practice of your profession. Even so, if you formulate a particular theory of counselling it should either be value-free or a clear indication should be given of how and in what way value systems interact with the model. If you are a psychologist, on the other hand, your personal values should not intrude upon either your data collection or the model you propose to interpret your data. An easy let-out in this situation is for the social scientist to say: With all these problems that face us we, unlike our fellows in the natural sciences, can no longer offer you value-free knowledge. But then they go on and unjustifiably extrapolate their predicament to *all* scientific knowledge and assert because they cannot, neither do they believe other disciplines can. Thus it soon becomes possible for them to dismiss the whole idea of value-free knowledge as a myth. This is a complete nonsequitur. What it points to is that there are aspects of social scientists' investigations, in so far as they are investigating other human beings, which make it particularly difficult to yield value-free knowledge.

Retaining the goal of value-free knowledge
To take the view of those who decry the possibility of value-free knowledge seems to ignore that it has already proved possible

to establish a considerable and ever-growing body of solid data about people. These data are available in medicine, physiology and in many branches of psychology, including the study of social behaviour. There can be little doubt that our personal limitations, together with some of our prejudices and the particular thought forms of the cultures in which we have grown up, can and have influenced our theory and biased, and at times distorted, our scientific endeavours. This, however, does not mean that we throw in the towel and abandon the belief that objectivity is attainable. Objectivity is evidenced all around us by the solid day-to-day evidence from the physical sciences as they guide our expectations and as we depend upon them for so many aspects of contemporary life. For the practice of science and the goals of science, the aim remains that of producing value-free knowledge. The fact that it is, and may continue to be, imperfectly attainable is beside the point. It still remains the norm and the goal at which we aim.

To reach this conclusion is not to forget the limited success of studies of how science has developed differently in different cultures. That alone, however, does not justify going completely over the top and saying that science's dependence on social factors is total and absolute. The faith of the scientist that there are regularities in nature and that they can begin to discover them remains entirely unscathed by the recognition that how they themselves work and how they formulate their generalities may well be a function of the society in which they live. If it was mistaken to take a dogmatic, positivist view in the past which said it was possible to hold a completely value-free conception of both the practice of science and the knowledge that it produced, so it is equally erroneous today to take the view, on limited evidence, that all science is value-laden. What has come under serious scrutiny and in some quarters been toppled from its pedestal is not science but *scientism*. Scientism emerges when science becomes an object of worship worthy of dedication for its own sake.

In so far as that erroneous view has been brought under scrutiny and toppled, science itself has been well-served.

The need for openness

In 1975 the President of the American Psychological Association, Donald Campbell, argued that psychologists' tendency at
that time to celebrate individual self-gratification and to depre-
cate traditional restraints encourages us to discard the wisdom
of social evolution. He argued that there is what he called
functional truth, in moral, religious and social traditions which
we ignore at our peril. Thus, said Campbell,

> If, as I assert, there is in psychology today a general background
> assumption that the human impulses provided by biological
> evolution are right and optimal, both individually and socially,
> and that repressive or inhibitory moral traditions are wrong, in
> my judgment this assumption may be regarded as scientifically
> wrong. . .Furthermore, in propagating such a background
> perspective in the teaching of perhaps 90% of college
> undergraduates (and increasing proportions of high school and
> elementary school pupils), psychology may be contributing to
> the undermining of the retention of what may be extremely
> valuable, social evolutionary inhibitory systems which we do not
> yet fully understand.[2]

In this way, Professor Campbell challenged the control beliefs
implicit in much of psychology at that time. The important thing
is that the science of behaviour should be content to be the
science of behaviour. It should contribute its insights into one
level of discourse, yet it should remain humble and unpretentious
enough to recognise that many of the deeply significant questions of life are not psychological questions and we ought not
to talk of them as if they were.

What is special about people?

Discussions of the place of values in science have introduced
their own special vocabulary. It has been suggested that there
are two characteristic features of human beings that make them
unique as subject matter for scientists, namely, *reflexivity* and
human values.

Reflexivity refers to the observation that human beings care
about the findings of the investigations that psychologists are
carrying out on them and reminds us that they have views about
them themselves. A piece of sodium is unaware that it is taking

part in an experiment, or that it is being deliberately studied. Indeed, if one were to tell the chemicals the outcome of a piece of research, their reactions next time round would be altered not one iota! On the other hand, if you tell the subjects of your psychological experiments what you are doing and why you are doing it, and then tell them the results of the experiment and repeat it, you may well find a different result the next time round.

As regards the human values involved, these will influence the perspective that the researcher chooses to take to the studies and this, by implication, will influence the findings that are reported. It is claimed that some of the models of humans implicit in a great deal of the research in psychology today are impoverished to the extent that they distort the best qualities of human beings. Some believe that it is actually dehumanising to think of people as if they were *only* reinforcement maximisers or information processors. The crux of this kind of critique is that if researchers entertain these stultified models of human beings as basic to the understanding of their research, then they will indeed accumulate scientific evidence that seems to support the belief embodied in the models with which they started their research. Another case of self-fulfilling prophecies.

We can readily agree with Koch about the dehumanising effect of slipping into what has been called 'nothing buttery': regarding man as 'nothing but' an information processor or 'nothing but' reinforcement maximisers. However, my impression is that most researchers, whether using information theory models or reinforcement models, are perfectly aware that these are models of limited applicability but that they remain important and helpful tools in the conduct of research.

We opened out this question right at the beginning and saw the danger of this sort of 'nothing buttery'. Whether many people are locked into it these days is debatable. I may be being unduly optimistic and you could show me why by reminding me of the way in which psychological jargon infiltrates everyday language, so that we too readily say that so and so was 'switched on' or was 'conditioned'.

Psychologists as unwitting agents for change

Perhaps there is a more telling comment on what is distinctive about psychological research from the point of view of scientific methodology and inference. Whilst psychologists in common with their fellow natural scientists not only collect data but seek to construct explanations of what they observe, they also consider what those they observe might become if they were made aware of the results of the research on them. Looked at in this way, psychologists should be seen as much as agents in the formation of human beings as researchers trying to understand how human beings work. I suspect that this sort of thing is happening already. We saw earlier that the typical scientist, say a pharmacologist, doesn't blindly experiment with every possible drug he can think of and observe its effects on human beings. Usually he is faced with particular problems in human disease or behaviour, be it hypertension or depression. He works towards producing specific drugs which will relieve the symptomatology of the disease. I suspect that something not dissimilar applies to the majority of psychologists in the way they go about their research. Writers such as Harré believe that we should have in the forefront of our research in psychology concepts such as personal power, agency and moral responsibility. If we do this, he claims, the progress of psychological research and its value for human beings will be advanced. It is an interesting and challenging view but the proof of the pudding will be in the eating. It is difficult for many of us to see how one moves from the fine statements of Harré and his colleagues and applies them to the actual planning and carrying out of research, at least in the more biological specialisations in psychology. Time will tell whether this sort of approach will ultimately be fruitful.

Earlier, and as an aside, we noted that despite his enduring influence, many of Freud's theories are no longer taken very seriously by his fellow psychologists, though there are many psychoanalysts who accord his theories greater worth. And yet there was a time when some regarded Freudian theories as 'scientific'. But that only raises the further question of how does one judge when an account is a scientific account. And then the further question arises of how scientific accounts of persons should be related to the more familiar accounts we give of ourselves and others in everyday language. What is the particular task of the scientist when he studies the mind and behaviour? How does he see his scientific accounts as related to the other more familiar everyday accounts?

Is the dignity of man threatened?

The account given in an earlier chapter of the several different levels at which man can be studied alerts us to the fact that the scientific approach to man, restricted for good reasons to particular levels, inevitably leads to losing sight of man as a whole. As Lipowski put it in his lecture referred to earlier, history teaches us 'That human behaviour cannot be explained or predicted from any single theoretical standpoint' and that 'We need to bring together facts and hypotheses from three mutually irreducible vantage points, the psychological, the biological and the sociological'.[3] We must put him together again at some point if we are not to finish up deceiving ourselves into thinking we have understood man. Sadly the tone of some reports of scientific approaches to the study of man are intemperate. They appear to threaten the dignity of man from the viewpoint of someone who regards him highly whether within a humanistic or a religious framework.

That a reductionist and/or materialist metaphysic necessarily follows from the scientific evidence would be seen as silly and illogical by some of the leading scientists working in the field today. Thus Sir John Eccles, Nobel Laureate and former Professor of Physiology at Canberra has written,

> Nor do I believe with the physicalists that my conscious experiences are *nothing but* the operation of the physiological mechanisms of my brain. It may be noted in passing that this extraordinary belief cannot be accommodated to the fact that only a minute amount of cortical activity finds expression in conscious experience. Contrary to this physicalist creed, I believe that the prime reality of my experiencing self cannot with propriety be identified with some aspects of its experiences and its imaginings—such as brains and neurones and nerve impulses and even complex spatio-temporal patterns of impulses.[4]

Or again, another Nobel Laureate in Medicine, Dr Roger Sperry, has written,

> The change is away from the mechanistic, deterministic and reductionist doctrines of pre-1965 science to the more humanistic interpretations of the 1970s. Or current views are more mentalistic, wholistic and subjectivist. They give more freedom in that they reduce the restrictions of mechanistic determinism and they are more quality rich and more rich in value and meaning.[5]

Later on he takes issue with a distinguished Australian philosopher when he writes, 'The new position directly opposes prior materialist doctrine that has been telling us for more than half a century that "Man is nothing but a material object, having none but physical properties" and that "Science can give the complete account of man in purely physico-chemical terms".[4] Sperry takes these quotes from the writings in the late 1960s of Professor Armstrong, whom he describes as a founding father and leader of the materialist, so-called mind-brain identity theory, which still today finds support, though with major reinterpretations to bring it into closer concordance with the causal emergent views of mind outlined above.

Some, to be sure, would caution the too-rapid advance of the scientific study of man. Their grounds would be varied and yet one cannot help but feel that behind them all there would be the vestiges of some aspects of the so-called Graeco-medieval tradition which even leads some today to champion an anti-technological bias—until they are personally in need of the fruits of technology in medical care. We could well use a quotation from the historian of science, Professor Hooykaas, and apply it to the study of man. Hooykaas, commenting on the ever-present danger of retreating from the healthy attitude of Francis Bacon, one of the founders of science, to a defensive and Graeco-medieval tradition, wrote:

> It is true that the results of our dominion over nature have been unhealthy in many cases; the powerful river of modern science and technology has often caused disastrous inundations. But by comparison the contemplative, almost medieval, vision that is offered as an alternative would be a stagnant pool.[6]

For those who feel that there is something very special about man, it is understandable that they view with concern, verging on antagonism, the attempt to dissect him, his mind and his behaviour, from a scientific point of view. At the same time, many who work in the field hope that their efforts can open up for man new vistas of life, health and achievement, if their findings are properly used.

— 7 —

The mind/brain link

Consciousness and personal freedom

Earlier chapters can have left little doubt that every new advance in the cognitive and neurosciences points to a tightening link between mind and brain. However, such a statement, if it ignores half the evidence, can give the impression that the mind and its activities are circumscribed, limited, determined or directed solely by the structures of the brain. In so doing one would be forgetting those other strands of evidence, equally relevant to a balanced assessment, which have underlined how the mind determines the activity of the brain.

To be selective and to concentrate exclusively on the evidence from the 'bottom-up' approach, when taken to its logical conclusion, can certainly raise worries about some of our cherished beliefs about our freedom and responsibility. To be sure there are many instances, and we have named some by way of illustration, of how a malfunctioning or disordered brain sets limits upon our freedom of thought and action. Parkinson's disease, some types of schizophrenia and Alzheimer's disease would be cases in point. But we are talking about the *normal* functioning of the mind and brain. There is, I believe, no refuge in the findings of neuroscience for those who wish to escape personal responsibility for their actions. Certainly it is my impression that the majority of those working at the coalface of neuroscience see good reason why, by studying man at different levels of scientific analysis, there is much to be learned that will enhance the overall understanding of ourselves and make clearer the true bounds of human freedom.

There is no point in making a virtue of guessing about the biological roots of our minds and our nature, when by sustained hard work we can secure a firmer base for such understanding. Such knowledge about the physical substrate of mind and personality can, in principle, provide us with a more profound understanding of why, for example, we speak and act as we do. Moreover, in practice such knowledge has the potential to enable us to act with more compassion and understanding towards those whose brains have become disordered. (Witness, for example, the exciting clinical trials undertaken in 1991 with the drug Cognex aimed at relieving some of the cognitive effects of Alzheimer's disease.) Of itself, such knowledge gathered by cognitive neuroscientists does nothing to make empty or superfluous notions of personal agency and individual responsibility. Professor J Z Young, a senior figure amongst British neurobiologists, reminded us recently that 'we cannot in the name of neuroscience (and I would add psychology) evade personal responsibility for the choices that we make'.[1]

For most of us, most of the time, the experience and awareness of our personal freedom is so self-evident and so all pervasive that any suggestion that we are under an illusion in thinking that we are free is easily discounted. And yet, it can be plausibly argued that the evidence we have reviewed and illustrated in the preceding chapters of the ever-tightening link between mind and brain, should make us pause and wonder whether there is not more in the suggestion that our freedom is illusory than we have thought in the past. Noting, as we have, that the brain is made up of physico-chemical components and that these work in a deterministic way, and noting that events in the brain seem to be reflected in events in mental activity, it is an easy step to believe that our impression of freedom of thought and action, self-evident though it is to each of us, may not be as firmly based as we would wish.

No easy answers

Philosophers down the centuries grappling with the puzzles surrounding the mind/brain link have come up with almost every conceivable solution. Materialists deny the reality of mind and see all behaviour as having solely physical causes. Idealists give primacy to mental phenomena. These alone truly exist. Yet others, whilst recognising and acknowledging the existence of mind and brain, construe their interrelation in different ways. Monists see the two as identical; some see them as different aspects of the same 'stuff'. Some dualists argue that the two are radically different and quite separate entities running along in parallel or causally interacting. The interaction for Descartes was in the pineal gland, for Eccles in the cerebral hemispheres. Many psychologists, following the lead given by Kenneth Craik, take what is called a 'functionalist' approach. For them, mental phenomena do not depend on the particular constitution of the brain but on how it is functionally organised. Some psychologists who are also cognitive neuroscientists believe, as we saw earlier in chapter four, that one should take account of what the brain is actually made of and learn from it in constructing one's models of mental processes. However, whatever approach is taken, all ultimately come up against the problem of consciousness.

The revival of consciousness

The time when a generation of psychologists could, with some success, foist on students of human behaviour a doctrinaire refusal to acknowledge human consciousness is mercifully past. As has been pointed out, such extreme behaviourism was tantamount to 'feigning anesthesia' since such behaviourists must themselves have had direct personal knowledge, which they would have been lying to deny, of the extent to which their own behaviour was not only accompanied but shaped by their conscious mental activity. A balanced behaviourism still has much to contribute to psychology. Behaviourism will, however, lose respect if it deliberately fails to reckon with the brute fact of consciousness in the case of human subjects and probably also in higher animals.

Extremes of behaviourism never really took root in the United

Kingdom as they did in much of North American psychology. This was probably due to the pervasive influence in the UK of the 'functionalist' approach of Kenneth Craik mentioned above. In the USA one of the most influential figures challenging the validity and scientific productivity of extreme behaviourism has been Roger Sperry.

Roger Sperry has spent a lifetime working with distinction at the frontiers of brain science, culminating in the award of the Nobel Prize in 1981. As he makes clear in his many writings he came slowly to his present views as he reflected on the changing scientific evidence. Starting in 1952, he somewhat tentatively began to suggest that conscious experience should be taken more seriously and given more weight in constructing models of the whole person as a mind/brain unity. He tells in his 1990 paper in *Brain Circuits and Functions of the Mind: Essays in Honor of Roger W Sperry* how when, as he put it, his 'unthinkable thought' continued to hold up despite continued re-examination, he 'risked' a trial-run publication in 1965 which 'might allow me to save face should it promptly be shot down'. But it was not, so four years later in 1969 he presented his views to the National Academy of Sciences in the USA.

Reading his 1990 statement I detect several features of Sperry's view which can best be presented in his own words.

1 'Consciousness is conceived to be a dynamic emergent property of brain activity, neither identical with nor reducible to, the neural events of which it is mainly composed.'

2 Consciousness exerts 'potent causal effects in the interplay of cerebral operations'.

3 'In a position of top command at the highest levels in the hierarchy of brain organisation, the subjective properties were seen to exert control over the biophysical and chemical activities at subordinate levels.'

4 He emphasises that 'conscious phenomena are not conceived as "nothing but" neural events'.

5 He admits that 'the term "interaction" for the psychophysical relation is perhaps not the best descriptively'.[2]

Against the prevailing views of the dominant materialist-behaviourist climate of opinion in psychology in the USA in the

1950s, Sperry sensed a change in the next decades so that 'Today one finds mentalists, dualists and psychophysical interactionists surfacing again in numbers after having been essentially silent and invisible for decades'.[3] But, as Sperry acknowledges, there are dangers in this. Some construe these changed views so as to justify and propagate things like occultism and astrology. I share these concerns and the evidence for such a re-emergence is already all too apparent. Elsewhere we have commented on occultism and related topics thus:

> For several reasons, most research psychologists and professional magicians (who are wary of the exploitation of their arts in the name of psychic powers) are skeptical: (1) in the study of ESP and the paranormal there has been a distressing history of fraud and deception; (2) most people's beliefs in ESP are now understandable as a by-product of the efficient but occasionally misleading ways in which our minds process information; (3) the accumulating evidence regarding the brain-mind connection more and more weighs against the theory that the human mind can function or travel separately from the brain; and, most importantly, (4) there has never been demonstrated a reproducible ESP phenomenon, nor any individual who could defy chance when carefully retested. After one hundred years of research, and after hundreds of failed attempts to claim a $10,000 prize that has for two decades been offered to the first person who can demonstrate '*any* paranormal ability', many parapsychologists concede that what they need to give their field credibility is a single reproducible phenomenon and a theory to explain it.[4]

The force of Roger Sperry's insistence on the importance of conscious phenomena is underlined by the examples of the work of cognitive neuroscientists like Michael Posner described in chapter four. I find Sperry's views exciting and up to a point compelling. However, I share his concern about the possible dangers of talk about the 'interaction' of mind and brain. Wrongly construed, such language may too readily open the door to smuggling in a new form of dualism by the back door. On balance, I prefer, if at all possible, to avoid talk of 'interactions' with the all too ready connotations of two different, separate sorts of 'stuff'. It hardly needs saying that as yet no one knows

the answer to the nature of the mind/brain link. Later in this
chapter I shall return and offer a way of thinking about it which
I hope gives proper weight to the available evidence from
psychology and neuroscience whilst avoiding talking about interaction.

Consciousness and computation
At the end of his influential book, *Mental Models*, Philip Johnson-Laird discusses consciousness and computation. He believes
that some people, possibly misunderstanding the intention of
computational models of mind, find a computational theory of
consciousness distasteful and potentially threatening to some of
our deeply held views about human nature. He seeks to be
reassuring. He writes:

> For many people, the computational theory of consciousness may
> be distasteful. Surely, they will say, the human mind is a
> transcendental creation, and any attempt to explain away its
> mystery and to reduce it to computation is a wicked
> travesty. . .They have misunderstood my argument. Of course,
> there may be aspects of spirituality, morality and imagination
> that cannot be modelled in computer programs. But these
> faculties will remain forever inexplicable. Any scientific theory
> of the mind has to treat it as an automaton. This is in no way
> demeaning or dehumanising, but a direct consequence of the
> computability of scientific theories. Above all, it is entirely
> consistent with the view that people are responsible agents.[5]

It is noteworthy that, on the one hand, he sees in the computational approach no denial of the reality of spirituality and
morality. On the other hand, he is quite clear that there is here
no escape from our role as responsible agents. Both these points
take up and underline conclusions emphasised repeatedly in this
book which we saw echoed by other workers at the neuroscience
coalface such as Roger Sperry, Sir John Eccles and J Z Young.

Where is the human person in all this?
As we reflect on the models sketched out in earlier chapters we
may ask, do they raise any deep non-scientific issues? Do they,
for example, affect our concept of the human person? More
specifically, how do we relate what we know of ourselves by

immediate experience to the sorts of things we are beginning to learn about ourselves as a mind/brain unity from brain science? Is our dignity at risk?

We all have first-hand experience of what it means to be a human being. What, we may ask ourselves, does it mean to be a person? First, I think, it means that we believe that each of us has a personal story to tell. For each of us it is a distinctive story. As Professor Cooper, a founding father of neural networks said at a recent international meeting on neural networks, 'Nothing in all this does anything to deny the uniqueness of every individual.' It is our story and nobody else's. Let us call it my *I story*. So I say, for example, 'I see this,' or 'I feel that,' or 'I believe this or that.'

The story given by neuroscientists and by psychologists is different. We have seen that it may be about psychological mechanisms, it may be about cognitive processes, it may be about cortical areas of the brain, it may be about columns of cells firing in the brain, it may be about neural networks, and so on. The stories from these different approaches make the working assumption (and it is no more than that) that for each fact of my 'I story', my conscious experience, there is some or possibly several 'brain stories'. These do not necessarily have to correspond in a one-to-one way. There may be several different patterns of neural activity at different times corresponding to the 'I story' that I give when I say, 'I am looking at your face.' These occur at the various levels of organisation described earlier.

Just what is the nature of this mysterious correlation between my personal 'I story' and the 'brain story'? I think we have to say, if we are honest, that it remains an open question. We have explored some of the varied contemporary scientific views concerning its nature. We have seen that views on how we interpret them differ between those equally familiar with the brain story and the psychological story. I have several times mentioned, for example, Dr Roger Sperry who has his own particular answer to this puzzle. Others would have a different answer.

Some, following in the tradition of Descartes, will speculate that somewhere in the brain there must be a special region which sustains a two-way interaction between the world of the brain and the world of the mind. Sir John Eccles appears to hold a variant of this view. Even so, I think it has its own problems. As far as I know there is no evidence to suggest that any part of the brain differs in its properties from other parts in such a way that it could be confidently identified as *the* place where the mind/brain interaction takes place; nothing to give a clue as to this mysterious link between brain processes and conscious experiences. For myself, rather than portraying an immaterial mind interacting with a material brain, I find it does justice to the available evidence to regard 'mind talk' and 'brain talk' as two ways of talking about distinguishable aspects of the same set of events: the levels of analysis approach of cognitive neuroscientists described above. To put it another way, 'mind talk', my 'I story', is embodied in the brain story much in the way that a computer programme is embodied in the hardware of the computer. If the hardware is damaged the programme won't run properly; if the brain is damaged certain mind functions may not run properly.

At the level of the working of its physical components there is no good reason to doubt that the brain is a fully determinate system. Indeed, in an important sense, we depend upon the physical reliability of the system and its components for the carrying out of our intended actions. But that does not mean that the mind is determined by the uncontrolled working of the neurones, chemicals, glia cells and so on of the brain. What is happening at that level, what we earlier described as downstream, will depend on what is happening upstream where the webs of interacting neural networks embody our thoughts, attention and so on. What initiates those remains a mystery, though past experience and dialogue with others are clearly crucially influential factors.

The late Professor Donald Mackay suggested some years ago that a helpful analogy in thinking about the mind/brain linkage may be taken from the ubiquitous computers of today's world. Thus when we set up a computer to solve a particular mathematical equation we may say that the behaviour of the computer is determined by the equation being solved. In other words, what the physical components of the computer do will depend upon the equation being solved. But at the same time a computer engineer would say, and quite correctly, that every physical event occurring in the computer is fully determined by the laws of physics as applied to the physico-chemical components of the computer. Notice that the computer engineer would be using the same word, *determined*, that we had used in the previous sentence when we said that the 'behaviour' of the computer is determined by the equation being solved. Is there a conflict here? No, any appearance of a conflict is illusory. What is more, we have no need to imagine that our computer is in some strange way open to non-physical influences (the mind?) in order that its behaviour may be determined by a non-physical equation as well as by the laws of physics. In other words, the two claims to determination, both of which are valid, both of which are correct, both of which are true, are not mutually exclusive claims. They are complementary claims.

Perhaps this analogy of the computer helps us to glimpse how the mind is in no sense secondary nor subservient to the physical activity going on in the brain. The way in which the mind determines the activity of the brain is just as real as the way in which the brain and its activity is determined by the laws of physics applied to its physico-chemical components. Thus the tightening of the link between mind and brain does not in any way minimise the importance of the mind or of mental activity. It does not mean that the mind is a mere epiphenomenon of the physical activity of the brain. The mind determines brain activity and behaviour. But in a complementary fashion the mental activity and the behaviour depend upon the physically determinate operations of the brain, itself a physico-chemical system. Thus when that system goes wrong, or is disordered, there are changes in its capabilities for running the system which we describe as the mind or mental activity. And likewise, if the mind or the mental activity results in behaviour of particular kinds, this in turn may result in temporary or chronic changes in the physico-chemical make-up and activity of the brain, its physical substrate. Thus this ever tightening link does not minimise the importance of the mind or the brain in this unitary complex system.

We are therefore thinking of mental activity as embodied in brain activity rather than as being identical with brain activity.

To go beyond this view and to adopt what is called a monist identity view is to confuse categories which belong to two different logical levels as we saw above when we described the levels of analysis approach of today's cognitive neuroscientists. There is nothing within brain science or within psychology which offers any justification for asserting that a monist identity view is more compatible with the evidence than the view we have outlined here. Professor Roger Sperry put it well: 'The laws of biophysics and biochemistry are not adequate to account for the cognitive sequencing of a train of thought.'[6] Professor J Z Young was making a similar point when he wrote: 'for the present we shall use the terminology that the brain contains programmes, which operate as a person makes selection among the repertoire of possible thoughts and actions.'[7] Note it is the person who makes the selection not the brain. One of the points that we have continually to be aware of is the danger of confusing talk about brains or machines and talk about persons. It is conscious cognitive agents who think. It is people, *not* brains, who make choices.

One cannot emphasise too strongly the dangers of sliding into a form of thinking about human beings which relegates the conscious cognitive agent to a second place, as Lipowski put it, of adopting 'the reductionist gospel'. The point simply is that all our knowledge of brains and minds and computers come only through our experience and activity as conscious agents. It is only in and through that experience that we gain specific or any other kind of knowledge and that means that the conscious agent has what philosophers call ontological priority. As Donald Mackay put it some years ago, 'Nothing could be more fraudulent than the pretence that science requires or justifies a materialist ontology in which ultimate reality goes to what can be weighed and measured, and human consciousness is reduced to a mere epiphenomenon.'[8]

No amount of use of analogies, however, of this or any other kind, can, for the time being, remove the sense of awe that one feels as one reflects upon one's own experience as an embodied conscious agent; a conscious agent, that is, with all one's capacities to interact in dialogue with other conscious agents. The sense of mystery, for me at least, remains untouched by any amount of brain science. The question remains: Is this capacity of persons to engage in dialogue with themselves and with other persons one of the properties which makes them so special? I think there is at least a clue here to what is special about being a person.

Logical relativity and freedom of choice

When our freedom is seen as an illusion it is usually on the grounds that if you add together the effects of our genes, environment, circumstances, brain processes and so forth, and if you were able to compute the collective effect of all of these, you would in principle be able to predict anyone's behaviour in any situation. The late Professor Donald MacKay addressed this particular issue on numerous occasions. He coined the term 'logical relativity' to refer to the fact that what a detached spectator can quite rightly believe about someone's future will in general be different from what the chooser and actor herself quite rightly thinks about her own particular bit of the future. The claim that the individual making the choice was under an illusion about her freedom implies that there was something else that she ought to have believed in making the choice. But if any belief other than her present one (which is that the outcome of everything is up to her) could somehow, by science-fiction, be injected into her brain, she would then no longer be in the state on which the prediction which everyone else holds was based. Only with her present beliefs will she fulfil her expectations as outside observers watch her. She certainly is not under any illusion.

The details of this argument by Professor MacKay are not easy to follow and relevant sources for an extended treatment of it are given at the end of this book. The logic takes time to follow but the effort is worthwhile. Professor MacKay was keen to call into question and dismiss the frequently made argument that because cause and effect operate in the mechanisms of our brains therefore our firm subjective conviction that we have freewill is an illusion. To quote from Professor MacKay's recently published Gifford lectures:

It becomes useful to recognise what I have called a principle of relativity such that when the observer, the super-scientist, is correct to believe what he believes about your state of conditional readiness, we can then ask, what is it that you would be correct to believe about it? Because you certainly would not be correct to believe his story. And what he is correct to believe is not that there is 'room' in the sense of vague wishy-washy, indeterminate, random relations between prior and later events in his mental activity, but that there are quite precise, corresponding, correlated connections between the way he thinks, evaluates and chooses and the immediate future of his state of conditional readiness. In that sense then, we have not just an uneasy, neutral cohabitation of the deterministic outside observer's view and the voluntaristic agent's view. The two fit as neatly as hand and glove.[9]

Other views

Other scientists, not in this case brain scientists, but physicists and mathematicians, have struggled with this same problem and their solutions differ somewhat from that of Professor MacKay. Dr John Polkinghorne writes of 'the perpetual puzzle of the connection of mind and brain'.[10] He points out that if you are a thorough-going reductionist the answer to this puzzle is easy, 'mind is the epiphenomenon of brain, a mere symptom of its physical activity'.[11] But as he further points out, 'the reductionist programme in the end subverts itself. Ultimately it is suicidal.'[12] It destroys rationality and thought is replaced by electro-chemical neural events. Such events cannot confront one another in rational discourse, they are neither right nor wrong, they just happen. Thus writes Polkinghorne: 'if our mental life is nothing but the humming activity of an immensely complexly connected computer-like brain, who is to say whether the programme running on the intricate machine is correct or not?'[13] And later he goes on: 'the very assertions of the reductionist himself are nothing but blips in the neural network of his brain. The world of rational discourse dissolves into the absurd chatter of firing synapses. Quite frankly, that cannot be right and none of us believes it to be so.'[14] In arguing in this way, Polkinghorne is echoing Professor J B S Haldane who many years ago wrote, 'If my mental processes are determined wholly by the motions of the atoms in my brain, I have no reason to suppose that my beliefs are true. . .and hence I have no reason for supposing my brain to be composed of atoms.'[15]

There are thus several ways of thinking about this problem and it will remain a puzzle for those of us involved to work at for many years to come. But

> until we know better how to integrate the activities of mind and brain let us at least hold fast to our basic personal experience of choice and responsibility without denying the neurological insight that our mental activity is incarnated in our brains. These are complementary aspects of the whole person, just as wave and particle are complementary aspects of light.[16]

Does chaos theory help?
Recently there has been much discussion in the scientific press about the science of chaos. This word is used to describe the irregular unpredictable behaviour of deterministic non-linear dynamic systems. This is not new and doesn't contain new fundamental physics. What is new is the realisation that many real world physical problems contain chaotic elements and the capability provided by modern high speed computers to simulate chaotic behaviour has provided fresh stimulation to the study of chaos with its wide ranging applications in physics, chemistry and biology.

Chaos theory is most often talked about in the field of mete-orology. Some claim that if chaology is taken to its logical extremes then all of our predictions about such things as global warming will, whether the best or the worst, ultimately be rendered meaningless since its central tenet is that there is no such thing as a reliable prediction. Best known of all is the so-called butterfly effect which says that an insect batting its wings and disturbing the air in China today can next month transform storm systems in New York or the temperature of London in August.

As popular writers have pointed out, chaos is to a certain extent what you make of it. Some see chaos theory as nothing less than that third great revolution in the physical sciences, and, like the two that went before, it refutes Newtonian principles. Such advocates would assert that the simplest systems are now seen to create extraordinarily difficult problems when it comes to predicability. They suggest that only a new kind of science could begin to cross the great gulf between knowledge of what one thing does, whether it be one water molecule, one set of heart tissue or one neurone of the brain and what billions of them will do. The relevance of this to our present discussion is that there are some who believe that ideas from chaos theory may assist in our grappling with the puzzles about processes in the brain. A *Scientific American* article on chaos published in 1986 closed with the words:

> Even the process of intellectual progress relies on the injection of new ideas and on new ways of connecting old ideas. Innate creativity may have an underlying chaotic process that selectively amplifies small fluctuations and moulds them into macroscopic coherent mental states that are experienced as thoughts. In some cases the thoughts may be decisions, or what are perceived to be the exercise of will. In this light, chaos provides a mechanism that allows for free will within a world governed by deterministic laws.[17]

Another scientist who has speculated about the possible relevance of chaos theory to problems of personal freedom is John Houghton, formerly Professor of Physics at Oxford and now Director General of the Meteorological Office in Britain. He notes that

> we have no doubt about our freedom to make choices; we are making them all the time. The choices are, of course, restricted by the structure of space and time. in which we exist. They are also constrained by our environment or our circumstances, and our behaviour is undoubtedly in some ways preconditioned by our upbringing and our past experience. But not entirely so; our freedom to choose is real. In particular, we are constantly faced with choices between good and evil and are only too well aware of a propensity to choose the evil rather than the good.[18]

Clearly there is nothing remotely 'scientific' about ignoring or minimising our primary experience that we make choices all the time. To try and pretend on any ideological reductionist grounds that the common human experience of freedom to choose is an illusion is blatant unscientific special pleading. It amounts to sweeping universally shared and agreed empirical data under the carpet.

A balanced view and the way ahead

It could be argued that the greater the knowledge we have of the biological foundations of our behaviour and of how what we do to ourselves affects the workings of the neural substrate of our minds, the more responsible we become for our actions. It seems to me that the appropriate attitude to adopt towards ourselves is to give primacy to the exercise of our personal freedom. Although it is sad to reflect how seldom we do that. Unfortunately, we readily blame the environment for our failures whilst being all too ready to take credit for our successes. When thinking of attitudes to others, there is surely wisdom in taking seriously some of the research outlined earlier which showed how people are significantly shaped by their social, environmental and cultural contexts. On this view, we should regard ourselves as agents responsible for our actions but always be ready to entertain the possibility that others have been unduly influenced by their social and physical environment and to make allowances accordingly.

Philip Johnson-Laird addressed his book, *Mental Models*, mentioned above, 'to anyone who is seriously interested in a scientific understanding of how the mind works'.[19] Nearly five hundred pages later, he concluded that 'Any scientific theory of the mind has to treat it as an automaton.' But, he went on, 'This is in no way demeaning or dehumanising, but a direct consequence of the computability of scientific theories. *Above all, it is entirely consistent with the view that people are responsible agents*'[20] (italics mine).

We need, however, to be vigilant. The reductionist trap is all too often set in our path. As Sperry put it: 'The meaning of the message will not be found in the chemistry of the ink.'[21] To fall into that trap would be akin to claiming that, for example, by analysing the composition and distribution of the paints of an artist's masterpiece we have thereby shown that it is after all 'nothing but' paint on canvas. If only we will stand back, see the whole, and get the picture into perspective we shall be able to appreciate the masterpiece for what it is. To study man, his mind and brain, scientifically is not necessarily to threaten the dignity of man. Properly used, such knowledge can enable us to treat one another with greater dignity and understanding. In the realm of psychiatry this theme was taken up in the lecture by Lipowski from which I quoted at the outset of this book. He said that 'neither brainless nor mindless psychiatry could do justice to the complexity of mental illness and to the treatment of patients. A comprehensive, biopsychosocial approach to our field is needed. . .'[22] And earlier in the same lecture, acknowledging the simplistic escape offered by reductionism, he commended the views of Wallace that 'both the biological and the psychological aspects of mind are real, different and not reducible to each other'.[23]

— 8 —

What then is man?

The spiritual aspect

Thinking Christianly about neuropsychological pictures of man

It comes as no surprise to discover that some of the most fruitful approaches to the understanding of man within science today are, as we saw in earlier chapters, multi-disciplinary. Man's continuity with the non-human primates and the rest of the animal kingdom is exploited to the full in trying to understand more of the mind/brain link. The neuroanatomist, the neurochemist, the neurophysiologist, the molecular biologist all have things to say which are integrated with the views of the neuropsychologists. It is the neuropsychologist, however, who tries to see how the results of investigations at these other levels affect the behaviour and performance of the *whole* organism. Ultimately man must be seen as a unity as well as a being who can be studied at several different levels or from different perspectives.

We noted in earlier chapters, when looking at the pictures or models of man constructed within the various neurosciences, that they summarise the efforts at analysis at several different levels. All the various levels are necessary if we are even to begin to do justice to the complexity of what confronts us. Thus the

119

science of man provides us with a spectrum of different accounts, each framed in categories appropriate to its own level or perspective. The key question remains of how these different scientific accounts may be properly related to one another and to our personal experience as human beings.

We have several times noted the explanatory poverty of a thoroughgoing reductionist model. It makes the basic assumption that in the end the only scientifically acceptable explanation will be found in terms of physical forces between molecules. Such an approach by definition rules out the accounts given by physiologists in terms of nerve impulses or neurotransmitters, or psychologists in terms of cognition, conditioning and learning, or of cognitive neuroscientists in terms of neural networks, and certainly rules out the account of the theologian in terms of aspirations for eternity and awareness of the love of God our heavenly Father. The thoroughgoing reductionist holds (as part of his world view) that all accounts other than his own are at best temporary expedients which ultimately are doomed to become superfluous when a full account can be given at the molecular level. However, as we also saw, the reductionist approach has from time to time come under attack from developments within science, most recently from chaos theory. As John Houghton has written,

> Chaos demonstrates that a system can possess complicated behaviour that emerges as a consequence of the simple non-linear interactions of only a few components. . .The interaction of components on one scale can lead to complex behaviour on a larger scale that in general cannot be deduced from knowledge of the individual components.[1]

For reasons I have given earlier, my impression is that a reductionist approach and its underlying presuppositions are recognised both within the scientific community and by philosophers as mistaken, simplistic and fallacious. Purely physical explanations in terms of molecules do not even have the necessary concepts for talking about some of the most important functions of man as a psychobiological unity. In this regard, the example we have used already of the computer solving a mathematical problem is helpful. In theory, it is possible to describe the computer in terms of molecules, the physical motions of particles or in terms of the operation of electronic components, but the mathematician would want to argue that these accounts simply cannot convey the understanding that he, the mathematician, has of the most important aspect of the computer's activity. The point is that it is possible for an explanation to be complete in its own terms, and at its own level, but not thereby to exclude or render superfluous other explanations given at different levels.

I have repeatedly sought to illustrate how, within psychology and neuroscience, we need a hierarchy of levels of investigation, and their appropriate categories of explanation, to even begin to do justice to what we find as we study man. As scientists we certainly do not spend our time trying to find gaps in the explanation we give at one level so that we can fit in an explanation from another level. The way to an integrated understanding of man is not to hunt for gaps in any particular scientific account so that we can fit in other accounts using other descriptive terms. Such other terms, whether they are mind, soul or whatever, are not to be fitted in this way. Shakespeare's profound insights into human nature, into what makes us tick, what motivates us, what, in a metaphoric sense, our hearts are captive to, are not any the less relevant because we also talk today about aspects of our nature in more precise scientific terms. What we need to do is learn how the accounts at different levels are related. It is not even that we translate what is happening at one level into what is happening at another. The descriptions we give are neither identical nor independent, they are complementary.

The changing scientific scene
In earlier chapters we have seen how views on the mind/brain link have changed down the centuries. The beliefs, albeit unscientific, of phrenologists that an individual's distinctive personality traits and mental skills are localised in the brain seemed to receive support when clinicians showed that circumscribed damage to particular parts of the brain resulted in specific difficulties in speaking and understanding language. This emphasis on localisation was then challenged and fell out of favour

only to return to prominence with the careful work of neurologists and neuropsychologists this century.

The neurophysiologists gave fresh impetus to attempts to localise particular and very circumscribed aspects of mental life to specialised groups of cells in the brain. We exemplified this by reference to studies of face processing. These, and similar studies by neurochemists investigating the neuropathology associated with some mental illnesses, are typical of what we have called the 'bottom-up' approach to the study of the mind/brain link.

At the other extreme, we noted the work of cognitive psychologists who, with elegant and ingenious research techniques, study particular mental skills such as reading, remembering, imaging, understanding language. For them the preferred models are in terms of 'modules' interconnected in an information processing system. Their models are constructed and tested without any necessary reference to the actual physical make-up of the brain. Computer modelling is a useful tool here and cognitive models have been tried out on computers. For such modelling the physical components of the computers being used are of no special importance. These we typify as the 'top-down' approaches.

For long there seemed little hope, or indeed desire, of bridging the formidable gulf between the 'bottom-up' and 'top-down' approaches. But along came cognitive neuroscientists with their concepts of neural networks. At last, it seemed, there was real hope of beginning to bridge the gulf between the 'bottom-up' and the 'top-down' approaches.

Coincidentally, the development of powerful new techniques for monitoring and visualising the activity of the brains of normal people whilst actually performing particular mental tasks showed that some systems within the brain but not others were active when particular mental tasks were being done. Thus the crucial importance of what the mind was doing for how and where the brain would be most active was underlined. Mind, as Roger Sperry had noted, was not an outmoded concept. No longer could it be relegated to the status of a mere epiphenomenon, as some extreme exponents of the 'bottom-up' approach had tried to do. Such a view may fit well with their reductionist/materialist philosophies—their personal world views—but it had to be made clear that it was an expression of a world view not a necessary deduction from scientific evidence. So after all, your mind does matter; it matters very much, as indicated also by Lipowski in his overview of current trends in psychiatry.

Finally, we noted that without recognising the influence of the environment, physical and social, we were dealing with an artificial abstraction. The mind/brain unity is influenced by environmental factors. If these go wrong in development through, for example, severe and prolonged starvation or through isolation from normal social interactions, long lasting and possibly irreversible changes may occur in brain structure and function. Moreover, what the mind does habitually may produce chronic changes in the physical substrate of the brain. Again the mind does matter. This comes as no surprise to the Christian who is well aware of how the focus of her attention and of what she chooses to stock the modules of her mind with has direct consequences for how she behaves and the sort of person she becomes. In this context, the Apostle Paul's words come readily to mind:

> Whatever is true, whatever is noble, whatever is right, whatever is pure, whatever is lovely, whatever is admirable—if anything is excellent or praiseworthy—*think* about such things.[2]

Stock the modules of your mind with these. And then '. . .put into practice'.

Man the paradox
At the beginning of the 17th century Pascal wrote, 'Man is but a reed, the weakest thing in nature: but he is a thinking reed.'[3] He continued, 'But if the universe would destroy him, man would still be nobler than the thing that kills him, for he knows that he is dying whereas the universe is unaware of the advantage it has over him.'[4] For Pascal 'all our dignity therefore consists in being able to think',[5] so that whilst 'by means of space the universe contains me and swallows me up as if I were a point; yet by thought I comprise the universe'.[6] The delicate balance of, on the one hand, man's greatness and, on the other, his lowliness, recurs frequently in Pascal's *Pensees* (1659). It is

also a theme finding an echo in Charles Darwin's *Descent of Man* (1871). Darwin wrote 'Man with all his God-like intellect which has penetrated into the movements and constitution of the solar system. . .with all these exalted powers. . .still bears in his bodily form the indelible stamp of his lowly origin.'[7]

The conflicting impressions of man's significance and yet of his insignificance confront us still today. Recently, I visited the UK telescopes built at the top of Monokea in Hawaii. Afterwards I was shown data just recorded which, as I was told, portrayed the collision of two galaxies which had occurred thirty million light years ago. In the face of such mind-boggling dimensions how truly insignificant man appears. And yet, it is man who is making these observations. It is man 'the thinking reed', who encompasses the universe and its workings with his mind. And the ability to do that depends, as we have seen repeatedly in preceding pages, on the efficient functioning of those ten to the tenth little cells that we have between our ears. Such reflections raise afresh the age old question that heads this chapter: 'What then is man?'

The answers given down the centuries to this seemingly simple question 'What is man?' were not given in a vacuum. Prevailing thought forms in succeeding centuries and different cultures mould and have been moulded by the answers given. The same is true for us in our generation. For us it is 'natural' to very readily interpret it as inviting an answer in terms of man's biological or psychological nature. When, however, the Psalmist posed the question, the context makes it clear that his concern was not with man's nature in terms of his biological ancestry, physical or psychological make-up, but rather in terms of his role, the purpose of his existence, his destiny. It is this wider context which Professor Hooykaas describes as a 'world view'. As he puts it, 'The Bible has a certain world view, that of the total dependence of the world on its Creator, but not a definite world picture.'[8]

Today, as then, within any particular 'world view' there is likely to be a diversity of pictures held of the details of man's biological links, physical make-up and psychological functioning.

World views and world pictures

As we saw in chapter six, no scientist goes about his work, nor reflects on it, in an intellectual vacuum. Whether we bring it out into the open or not, we all possess what may be called a 'world view'. By this we mean a set of fundamental beliefs about the ultimate nature of reality. When probed, these are found to say significant things about both the physical and non-physical aspects of life. They reveal what a person believes about the relation of the physical world to any deity he believes in. They say things about the ultimate source of existence, about the value of the world and its inhabitants, and about the purpose of the world's existence. It is these world views which come into play when we discuss questions of meaning and significance.

Such world views can be usefully distinguished from 'world pictures'. The latter refer to particular conceptual models we have devised of the workings of some aspects of the physical world. A world picture, unlike a world view, is not concerned with ultimate matters of a metaphysical or religious kind. To ask if the earth revolves around the sun is to pose a question about a world picture. To ask if the sun is a divine being, a serious question in times past, and still for some primitive peoples today, is a question about a world view. Likewise, to ask a question about how mental activity depends upon brain activity is a world picture question, but to ask whether man is made in the image of God is a world view question.

We need to note that on almost any topic there are at any time several world pictures for us to choose from. They have changed over the centuries. In general, by their nature, such world pictures are not permanent. Our contemporary set of world pictures has been formulated primarily on the basis of research using the experimental and observational methods of science.

Confusion easily arises when world views are smuggled into world pictures and presented as if they were an intrinsic part of those world pictures when in fact they are philosophical or metaphysical presuppositions which are not derivable in any logical sense from the science that has helped to make up the world picture.

Presuppositions and interpreting the mind/brain link

Those of us who work in psychology and neuroscience also have our presuppositions. There is the ever present temptation to intrude a particular world view, whether religious or reductionist/materialist, into our interpretation of the ever tightening link between brain and mind. This was well illustrated in the report of a conference held in 1990 under the title, *Atom in the Mind.*

Commenting on the contributions by John Polkinghorne and Sir John Eccles the report said,[9]

> Eccles clothed the advocacy for dualism that has always characterised his work, in the latest neurophysiological discoveries. On this occasion he chose the bundling of pyramidal cell axons into what he termed 'dendrons'. These, according to Eccles, are the cortical site of 'psychons'. These are discrete components of conscious experience and intervene in the action of dendrons at the quantum level. This is the gateway for the mind to intervene in the brain that Eccles has been advocating since the 1970s and Cartesian devotees have been advocating since the seventeenth century. Though relocated from valves in the pineal gland to synapses in layers three and four of the cortex, the story is the same and the objections that troubled Descartes position are likewise a problem for Eccles.

> Polkinghorne was able to increase the definition of an important question that lay behind many contributions throughout the day, how to frame the replacement for reductionism that is now so clearly signalled. He noted that equations for the behaviour of physical systems in isolation are the tail rather than the dog of natural causality. Patterns of emergent downward causation are what moves the world of matter, especially in organic systems like the brain. The enormous complexity of organic structures renders their sensitivity to initial conditions far greater than, say, weather systems which are now known to be inherently unpredictable. It is just this sort of point that is made elsewhere by physicists, thermodynamicists, neuropsychologists and evolutionists. Collectively, these indicate the real opportunity that now exists for progress on non-reductionist theories of mind.

The report also pointed out that reductionists have beliefs and presuppositions. Thus, in summarising the contributions at the conference, the author wrote,

Some, like Eccles, were honestly religious. Some, like Blakemore, were religious but didn't know it (Blakemore's Science being his Faith). Some, like Polkinghorne, were sufficiently at ease within both arenas of belief that they could offer some way forward. Indeed, the contrast between these three is striking. Eccles knows what he wants to find in the brain. Blakemore knows what he doesn't want to find. However, both agree that the way forward is to look into smaller and smaller details. Whether it be Eccles' search for mystery or Blakemore's effort to eliminate it, the character of the inquiry is the same. Polkinghorne, by contrast, seems open on how the brain's action is directed and is happy to consider that significant causes emerge at a systems level. These different attitudes reflect the rigidity or otherwise of the link between epistemology and ontology. When rigid, as in the case of Blakemore and Eccles, then the resulting research deals in absolute properties, tightly coupled to objects with definite locations in space. Within Polkinghorne's more flexible regime, relational and systems properties become admissible. The way ahead must lie with this more open ontological stance.

The world view which informs my own thinking about man and his nature is like Polkinghorne's, a Christian one. However, the world view of Sir John Eccles is also a Christian one though, as is evident from the report cited above, that does not mean that his world picture on the mind/brain link is the same as that of Polkinghorne. In the context of our present discussion there are features of a Christian world view of our human nature which are relevant and timely whatever world picture we espouse. We must consider these now.

Human nature within a Christian world view
What sort of answer does the Bible give to the question 'What is man?' In the classic passage of Psalm 8 it is at once evident that the context of the enquiry is quite different from that of the investigations reviewed in earlier chapters. There our concern has been with what man believes about the scientific make-up of his own nature. In Psalm 8 the context makes it clear that the central concern is the question of the significance of man as he stands before his creator and sustainer.

This is not the place, even if I were competent to do so, to summarise the many things that Christians have said about man and his nature. That does not mean, however, that we cannot spell out the essential features of what the Bible says on this topic. To do so means recognising that running through the varied accounts there are certain recurring features.

First, in a very profound sense, it is a timeless view. It made sense to our forbears long before science appeared; it said important things about themselves relevant to their daily living. That alone should warn us against misconstruing it today by trying to impose on its vocabulary a precision, familiar to us today within science, which it was never intended to have. We also discover that its main concern is with what God thinks about man. It has little interest in one person's analysis of another person's nature. It is a God-centred view and is preoccupied with the relationship of man to God. It seems primarily concerned to give us advice and enduring truths on how to live our lives day by day.

It is abundantly clear that the various terms used to talk about man in the Bible, and there are many, are not those we expect to find within contemporary experimental science. It does not talk about species, it talks about people; it is not biological, it is biographical. It is not concerned with the properties of human beings whether physiological, biochemical or psychological (in the scientific sense) but is concerned with how people act in history. It is also evident that a variety of pictures are given to us in the library of books contained in the Bible. Each enriches the common theme and as such amplifies what is given elsewhere.

From the variety of pictures given, certain common features emerge. From the opening pages of Scripture there is a contrast between man seen as the summit of God's creative acts and man as very firmly a part of creation. Man is made from the dust of the ground and like other living creatures, he becomes a living creature. His creatureliness is highlighted over and over again: 'you are from dust and you will return to dust'; or as the psalmist put it, 'He knows how we were made, he knows full well that we are dust' (Psalm 103:14). We must never forget our intrinsic mortality. The Apostle Paul reminds Timothy that 'God only hath immortality' (1 Tim 6:16). Pascal put the balanced view so well all those years ago when he wrote:

> It is dangerous to show man too clearly how much he resembles the beast without at the same time showing him his greatness. It is also dangerous to allow him too clear a vision of his greatness without his baseness. It is even more dangerous to leave him in ignorance of both. But it is very profitable to show him both.[10]

In trying to fill out something of the mystery of what it is to be a human being the Old Testament writers identify several aspects of personhood. They emphasise that man is physically alive, a living creature, a tangible material being. In this context, the word 'soul' is frequently used. Even so, the many different ways in which it is used seem to defy any attempt to give a precise definition and consistent usage. The writers are concerned with the way in which human beings act and react to one another; what happens when people become weary, when they become covetous, when riches are denied. When talking about man's actions and reactions, frequently the word 'heart' is used. Yet, lest one is tempted to give this a single precise meaning, you immediately find occasions when the words 'heart' and 'soul' are used interchangeably. In addition, there is an aspect of man which may be loosely defined as *the spiritual aspect*. This very important intangible quality gives to man his special significance. It seems that if you can say something about this aspect of man, you reveal something of what he is really like; you say what it is that inspires him for his daily living. Know what a man or woman set their hearts on and you know a good deal about their essential character, their spiritual dimension.

As you move to the New Testament there is a more extensive treatment of man and his nature. But that does not mean that a more precise model can be constructed. The words used there carry different meanings in different contexts and in the hands of different authors. There are, however, two generalisations that can be made about the New Testament picture of man. First, like the Old Testament, it emphasises the unity of man. Man is a psycho-physical or somato-psychic unity. Moreover, he is a unity in this present earthly life, and he will be a unity in some

new form in the new heavens and the new earth to which he
looks forward. However, being a unity does not mean that one
cannot usefully distinguish between aspects of his nature—of
his physical and psychological make-up. The New Testament
offers several pictures which prompt us to think more deeply
about ourselves and the mystery of what it is to be human. At
times the physical aspect of man as a living being is emphasised,
at times his psychological aspect is emphasised, and at yet other
times the moral and spiritual aspects are emphasised.

In the New Testament, as in the Old, the spiritual aspect of
man receives extensive treatment. But again, spirituality is not
an abstract quality. True, it is in part revealed in what a person
says he believes about God and about his fellow humans, what
he claims are his goals in life. Equally, it shows in what he
endows with greatest worth, and what he shows are his moral
priorities. It is embodied in what he does, how he treats other
people, how he treats the created universe. Indeed, in a sense,
we may note that just as we have seen that mental activity or
the mind is embodied in the physical workings of the brain, so
the spiritual aspect of a person is embodied in his activities as
a mind/brain unity.

Commenting on past debates about the spiritual aspect of a
person in the Christian tradition, the authors of *What then is
Man?* wrote helpfully, 'The word "spirit" is used over and over
in the sense of what might be termed the operational content
and direction of man's thoughts, words and actions.' And that,
'spirit, then, is a fruit, an outcome of the individual's life and
experience'. They went on: 'If spirit is regarded as a functional
outcome rather than a separate structural entity, the difficult and
troublesome trichotomy theory becomes entirely unnecessary.'[11]

In similar vein, a more recent book by Dallas Willard (1988)
contains the following paragraph:

> Spirituality in human beings is not an extra or 'superior' mode
> of existence. It's not a hidden stream of separate reality, a
> separate life running parallel to our bodily existence. It does not
> consist in special 'inward' acts even though it has an inner
> aspect. It is, rather, a relationship of our embodied selves to God
> that has the natural and irrepressible effect of making us alive
> to the Kingdom of God—here and now in the material world.[12]

This brief digression into a layman's view of the essential features of a Christian view of human nature will raise at least two questions in the minds of fellow Christians who read it. First, how does it all relate to what Christians believe about life after death? Second, whatever happened to the soul?

What about life after death?
It is natural for some Christians when first becoming aware of the strength of the case for seeing man as a mind/brain unity to sense a conflict with their long held beliefs about life after death. It is often said that Western thought is still unwittingly pervaded by Greek-Hellenistic ways of thinking. In this context, that may mean it is natural to think about each of us as possessing an immortal soul which leaves our mortal body at physical death. Such a view, however, is not the one which dominates the Bible's way of talking about our nature. As we saw above, we are warned in Scripture never to forget our intrinsic mortality. We referred to Paul's letter to Timothy, where he emphasised that 'God only hath immortality' (1 Tim 6:16). But if that is so, what about our Christian conviction of life after physical death?

In the context of our concerns in this book I think two comments are timely. First, that the Bible's emphasis is on resurrection not immortality. Jesus is recorded as saying that 'those who have done good will rise to live, and those who have done evil will rise to be condemned' (John 5:29), and all this in response to God's activity, not as a natural property of their make-up. Paul in the classic resurrection passage in his first letter to the Christians at Corinth (chapter fifteen) spoke repeatedly of our hope of life after physical death resting on the resurrection of Jesus. Moreover, in his pictures of what this mystery might mean he emphasised continuity with change. So the seed which is sown is given 'its own body' (1 Cor 15:38). 'The body that is sown is perishable, it is raised imperishable. . .It is sown a natural body, it is raised a spiritual body' (1 Cor 15:42, 44). These and similar pictures help us to glimpse enough to be at peace. I, personally, find the Apostle's use of the picture of death as sleep most helpful. We must not press it too far. But it does suggest that, as when we go to sleep there follows a passage of time and then a fresh awareness of a new day, so will be our passing from physical death to resurrection life. And as in sleep our physical embodiment, the chemistry of our make-up, will have changed, but we are convinced of our continuing identity when we wake up, so it will be in life after physical death.

My second comment, and again it is a personal one, is that I find the computer analogy used earlier helpful. What I mean is this. The same computer programme can, in principle and in practice, run on a number of different computers, each made of different physical components. If I imagine the super computer programmer who writes a programme which captures the 'essential me' then whilst at present it runs in seventy-six kilograms of wobbling protoplasm, one day it will run in a new embodiment glimpsed in the biblical references to a 'spiritual body' and 'a glorified body'. Glimpses only, but enough. All this is not an argument for life after death; that we hold by faith. It is simply to say that nothing I have set down elsewhere in this book, writing about human nature as a scientist, makes it more difficult for me to believe in what is promised in Christ. Rather, if anything, for me at least, it makes it easier to think about as I add analogies from science to the metaphors of the seed and the plant from Scripture.

Whatever happened to the soul?
It is the most natural thing in the world when discussing our nature to talk about souls and bodies. Moreover, it seems perfectly 'natural' when talking about the possibility of life after death to refer to immortal souls and/or the continuing existence of disembodied spirits. These 'natural' ways of thinking and talking are part of Western civilisation's rich heritage from Greek philosophy, especially Platonism. So 'natural' have such ways of thinking and talking become that they are readily and, perhaps, unthinkingly, used by Christians when expressing their Christian hope. This is not surprising since Platonism has undoubtedly been a powerful and formative influence on developing Christian thought. What is not so readily remembered is that, as briefly spelled out above, Christianity grew more directly out of ancient Judaism. From there it received the idea of resurrection, as the Apostle's Creed makes clear. Despite this

central tenet of Christian belief stressing the psycho-physical unity of man, seeing man as 'an animated body, and not an incarnated soul', it is still common to think of a person as non-material spirit inhabiting a physical organism.

Certainly nothing that has been written so far in this book denies or makes superfluous the many truths and rich insights that are given in the Bible's ways of talking about our nature, some of which we sketched out earlier in this chapter. We noted there that there is a long catalogue of terms used—mind, body, soul, spirit, heart and so on—and each, in its context, conveys profound insights into the mystery of what it is to be a human person.

The Bible likewise also identifies many parts of the body as the organs of emotions, for example, liver, kidneys, intestines, uterus, bones and so on. Interestingly, in the context of this book the nervous system and the vascular system are not mentioned! The word 'soul', we are told, etymologically is connected with the throat, probably involves the respiratory system and is the centre of the emotional and sentient life rather than of the rational and moral. Certainly the Old Testament uses no word for brain. There the heart is the organ of thought—a natural place as we saw in our brief opening historical review.

But what of the soul in the New Testament? As we saw above, Christian teaching traditionally divided man into body, soul and spirit, the 'troublesome trichotomy theory' referred to earlier. This certainly generates problems since close study shows that the differences, if any, between soul and spirit are not easy to define. Basically, the New Testament sees a man as consisting of a body (*soma*) and a soul (*psyche*). Though both taken together comprise the complete person as a unity, it is nevertheless possible to say that man has a body (e.g., 2 Cor 5:6) but is a soul or living being (1 Cor 15:45). The difficulty of distinguishing between the soul and the spirit arises in part from the differing vocabularies of the New Testament writers. Paul, for instance, uses *pneuma* (for man's spirit) widely, but hardly ever uses *psyche*. John, on the other hand, never applies *pneuma* to man. All this adds up to the need to exercise caution when tempted to make dogmatic statements about what the soul is and does. Perhaps it would be prudent to follow the advice of one author who wrote: 'In terms of biblical psychology, man does not have a "soul" he is one. He is a living and vital whole. It is possible to distinguish between his activities, but we cannot distinguish between the parts, for they have no independent existence. . .'[13] Such a view is echoed in the recent *New Dictionary of Christian Theology* where we read: ' "Soul" (a word used sparingly in modern translations of the Bible) is not a part of human nature *but characterises it in its totality*, just as "flesh" and "spirit" do. A separate or different origin for "soul" no longer enters the picture' (my italics).[14]

So in answer to our question, 'Whatever happened to the soul?', we discover that in contemporary translations of the Bible every attempt is made to steer us away from making the soul into a thing, a separate entity. Rather, we are encouraged to recognise that it refers to the whole living person. Thus, whereas in Luke's gospel chapter twelve and verse nineteen we used to read 'And I will say to my soul; soul. . .' we now read in, for example, the New English Bible, 'And I will say to myself; "Man. . ." ', or in the New International Version, 'And I'll say to myself; "You. . ." '.

It is the whole person, already enjoying new life in Christ, who looks forward with confidence because, since Christ is risen, we also shall be raised with him. Embodied now, we shall be embodied then, clothed in a 'glorified body', a 'spiritual body'. But above all we are assured that we shall be like him and what more could we hope for?

There is hope
We acknowledge the combined effects on each of us, as a mind/brain unity, of our distinctive genetic endowments; of our early experience and upbringing; of our environment both imposed and self-generated; of how we exercise our capacity as responsible agents for the filling of our minds and the directing of our behaviour. Recognising these diverse influences can, I believe, have the good effect of generating in each of us a fresh resolve to be compassionate to those distressed in mind and to show a deeper understanding of their problems and struggles, and encourages us to help in every way possible.

No slick simplistic answers to the question 'What then is

man?' will do. For those of us engaged in research into the mind/brain link there is certainly strong motivation to push the frontiers of knowledge back in the hope and belief that solidly based scientific understanding of how the mind/brain unity functions holds out the best hope for alleviating the distress and suffering of the brain damaged and mentally ill.

As regards our concerns about our own situation, and at times our perplexity about the human condition, for those of us who are Christians there is hope. Mindful of our strivings and despite our all too frequent shortcomings, we can still confidently echo the words of Pinnocchio who, when floundering in self-doubt and struggling to justify himself, turned to his maker, Gepetto, and confessed , 'Pappa, I am not sure who I am. But if I'm all right with you, then I guess I'm all right with me.' As Christians we know that God loves us and accepts us in spite of what we are. We believe that no man has any ground on which to stand except God's grace. And that, we believe, abounds.

Endnotes

Chapter 1

1 *Joint Resolution* presented in the House of Representatives in the US Congress March 8, 1989 to designate the decade beginning January 1, 1990 as the 'Decade of the Brain'.
2 'Psychiatry: Mindless or Brainless, Both or Neither', the First Distinguished Member Lecture presented at the 38th Annual Meeting of the Canadian Psychiatric Association, September 28, 1988, by Professor Z J Lipowski. Published in the *Canadian Journal of Psychiatry* 34(3), 1989, pp. 249–254.
3 Oliver Sacks, *The Man Who Mistook his Wife for a Hat* (London: Pan, 1986) p. 22, 23, 24.

Chapter 2

1 Quoted by K M Heilman and E Valenstein, 'Introduction', in K M Heilman and E Valenstein, eds, *Clinical Neuropsychology* (Oxford: OUP, 1979) p 7, and taken from H Head, *Aphasia and Kindred Disorders of Speech* (Cambridge: CUP, 1926).
2 'Asymmetries of the Brains and Skulls of Non-Human Primates' in, Stanley D Glick, *Cerebral Lateralisation in Non-Human Species* (Orlando: Academic Press, 1985) chapter 10.
3 Michael I Posner, Steven E Petersen, Peter T Fox, Marcus E

Raichle, 'Localization of Cognitive Operations in the Human Brain, *Science*, 17 June 1988, Vol. 240, pp. 1627–1631.

4 Doreen Kimura, 'Monthly fluctuations in sex hormones affect women's cognitive skills', *Psychology Today*, November 1989, pp. 63–66.

5 Patricia S Churchland and Terrence J Sejnowski, 'Perspectives on Cognitive Neuroscience, *Science*, 4 November 1988, Vol. 242, pp. 741–745.

6 D R Humphrey and H J Freund, eds, *Motor Control: concepts and issues* (Chicester: Wiley, 1991). The quotations are from the chapter by Dr M Goldberg, pp. 249–250.

7 Mortimer Mishkin and Tim Appenzeller, 'The Anatomy of Memory', *Scientific American*, 256(6), 1987, pp. 62–71.

Chapter 3

1 Z J Lipowski (lecture), 'Sight and Insight: Regional Cerebral Metabolic Activity in Schizophrenia Visualised by Positron Emission Tomography, and Competing Neurodevelopmental Perspectives', in John L Waddington, *British Journal of Psychiatry*, 156, 1990, pp. 615–619.

2 Quoted by Z J Lipowski in 'Organic Mental Disorders: their history and classification, with special reference to DSM III', in N E Miller and G D Cohen, eds, *Clinical Aspects of Alzheimer's Disease and Senile Dementia* (New York: Raven Press, 1981) pp. 37–59.

Chapter 4

1 David Marr, *Vision* (San Francisco: W H Freeman, 1982).

2 Churchland and Sejnowski, 'Cognitive Neuroscience'.

3 R W Sperry, 'Psychology's Mentalist Paradigm and the Religion/Science Tension', *American Psychologist*, August 1988, pp. 607–613.

4 P Smolensky, 'On the proper treatment of connectionism', *Behavioural and Brain Sciences*, 11, 1988, pp. 1–23.

5 F Crick, 'The recent excitement about neural networks', *Nature*, 337, 1989, pp. 129–132; see also P S Churchland and T J Sejnowski, 'Neural Representation and Neural Computation', in Nadel, Cooper, Culicore and Hornisla, eds, *Neural Connections, Mental Computation* (Mass.: MIT Press, 1989), pp. 15–49.

6 Posner et al., 'Cognitive Operations'.

7 Michael I Posner and Steven E Petersen, 'The Attention System

of the Human Brain', in *Annual Review of Neuroscience*, 13, 1990, pp. 25–42.
8 Sperry, 'Mentalist Paradigm', p. 609.
9 Panti Kanerva, *Spatial Distributed Memory* (Mass.: MIT Press, 1988).
10 Churchland and Sejnowski, 'Cognitive Neuroscience'.

Chapter 5

1 Ann M Clarke and A D B Clarke, *Early Experience: Myth and Evidence* (London: Open Books, 1976).
2 *Health and Lifestyle Survey* (London: Health Promotion Research Trust, 1987) p. 212.
3 M E P Seligman, *Helplessness: On depression, development and death* (San Francisco: W H Freeman, 1975).
4 For examples of the work of E J Langer and J Rodin see 'The effects of choice and enhanced personal responsibility for the aged: A field experiment in an institutional setting', *Journal of Personality and Social Psychology*, 34, 1976, pp. 191–198; and 'Long-term effects of a control-relevant intervention with the institutionalized aged', *Journal of Personality and Social Psychology*, 35, 1977, pp. 897–902.
5 David G Myer, *The Human Puzzle* (San Francisco: Harper and Row, 1978).
6 Lipowski, 'Mindless or Brainless'.

Chapter 6

1 H J Van Till, R E Snow, J H Stek, D A Young, *Portraits of Creation* (Grand Rapids: Eerdmans, 1990).
2 Professor Donald Campbell's Presidential address to the American Psychological Association entitled, 'On the conflicts between biological and social evolution and between psychology and moral tradition', *American Psychologist*, 30, 1975, pp. 1103–1126.
3 Lipowski, 'Mindless or Brainless'.
4 For an amplification of Sir John Eccles' views and those of other neuroscientists see, for example, John C Eccles, *Brain and Conscious Experience* (Heidelberg: Springer-Verlag, 1966).
5 Sperry, 'Mentalist Paradigm'.
6 R Hooykaas, *Religion and the Rise of Modern Science* (Edinburgh and London: Scottish Academic Press, 1971)

Chapter 7

1 J Z Young, *Philosophy and the Brain* (Oxford: OUP, 1987).
2 Roger W Sperry, 'Forebrain Commissures and Conscious Awareness', in Colwyn Trevarthen, ed., *Brain Circuits and Functions of the Mind: Essays in Honour of Roger W Sperry* (Cambridge: CUP, 1990), from pp. 382–385.
3 Sperry, *Brain Circuits*, p. 383.
4 David G Myers and Malcolm A Jeeves, *Psychology Through the Eyes of Faith* (San Francisco: Harper and Row, 1988) p. 42.
5 P N Johnson-Laird, *Mental Models* (Cambridge: CUP, 1983) p. 477.
6 Sperry, 'Mentalist Paradigm', p. 609.
7 J Z Young, *Philosophy*, p. 19.
8 Donald M Mackay, *The Open Mind* (Leicester: IVP, 1988) p. 80.
9 Donald M Mackay, *Behind the Eye* (Leicester: Blackwell, 1991).
10 J C Polkinghorne, *One World* (London: SPCK, 1986) p. 92.
11 Polkinghorne, *One World*, p. 920.
12 Polkinghorne, *One World*, p. 92.
13 Polkinghorne, *One World*, p. 92.
14 Polkinghorne, *One World*, p. 93
15 JBS Haldane, *Possible Worlds* (London: Chatto and Windus, 1945) p. 209.
16 Polkinghorne, *One World*.
17 J P Crutchfield, J D Farmer, N H Parkhard North and R S Shaw, 'Chaos', *Scientific American*, 1986, pp. 38–49.
18 John Houghton, *Does God Play Dice?* (Leicester: IVP, 1988) p. 123.
19 Johnson-Laird, *Mental Models*, p. xiii.
20 Johnson-Laird, *Mental Models*, p. 477.
21 Sperry, 'Forebrain Commissures', p. 385.
22 Z J Lipowski, 'Mindless or Brainless'.
23 E Wallace, 'Mind body: monistic dual aspect interactionism', in *Journal of Nervous and Mental Disorders*, 176, 1988, pp. 1–20.

Chapter 8

1 J T Houghton, 'New Ideas of Chaos in Physics', in *Science and Christian Belief*, 1, 1989, pp. 41–51.
2 Philippians 4:8.
3 Pascal, *Pensées* (1659) fragment 347.
4 Pascal, *Pensées*, fragment 348.
5 Pascal, *Pensées*, fragment 347.
6 Pascal, *Pensées*, fragment 348.

7 Charles Darwin, *The Descent of Man*, 2nd edn (London, 1874) p. 619.

8 R Hooykaas, *Religion and the Rise of Science* (Edinburgh and London: Scottish Academic Press, 1971) p. 16.

9 From *Atom in Mind*, Newsletter of the History and Philosophy of Psychology Section of the British Psychological Society, 1990.

10 Pascal, *Pensées*.

11 *What then is Man?* (St Louis: Concordia Publishing House, 1958) p. 319.

12 Dallas Willard, *The Spirit of the Disciplines* (San Francisco: Harper and Row, 1988) p. 31.

13 J K Howard, *Faith and Thought*, 98, 1970, p. 163.

14 *New Dictionary of Theology* (Leicester: IVP, 1988) p. 653.